'Comprehensive, authoritative, accessible. This book is all that and more. There are issues and solutions in here that I never thought about in over twenty years of teaching and writing about this topic. It's a book that every human resources manager is going to want to have handy.'

– *Christine Burns MBE, author,*
E&D consultant and transgender activist

'A brilliantly succinct yet thorough book of which every business, big or small, private or public, should have a copy. So many questions answered and so much practical help contained. An absolute gem of demystification.'

– *Juno Roche, writer, campaigner and*
co-founder of TransWorkers UK

'A refreshing addition to the literature for corporate personnel and HR departments. Kermode and Fae demonstrate a sensitivity not just to their researched experiences of trans people, but also to the needs of employers.'

– *Previn Karian, editor,* Critical & Experiential:
Dimensions in Gender and Sexual Diversity

Employees in the Workplace

A Guide for Employers

of related interest

Can I tell you about Gender Diversity?
A guide for friends, family and professionals
CJ Atkinson
Illustrated by Olly Pike
ISBN 978 1 78592 105 6
eISBN 978 1 78450 367 3
Can I tell you about...? series

Trans Voices
Becoming Who You Are
Declan Henry
Foreword by Professor Stephen Whittle, OBE
Afterword by Jane Fae
ISBN 978 1 78592 240 4
eISBN 978 1 78450 520 2

An Employer's Guide to Managing
Professionals on the Autism Spectrum
Marcia Scheiner (Integrate Autism Employment
Advisors) with Joan Bogden
Illustrated by Meron Philo
ISBN 978 1 78592 745 4
eISBN 978 1 78450 513 4

Employees in the Workplace
A Guide for Employers

Jennie Kermode

With additional material by Jane Fae

Jessica Kingsley *Publishers*
London and Philadelphia

First published in 2018
by Jessica Kingsley Publishers
73 Collier Street
London N1 9BE, UK
and
400 Market Street, Suite 400
Philadelphia, PA 19106, USA

www.jkp.com

Library of Congress Cataloging in Publication Data
Names: Kermode, Jennie, author.
Title: Transgender employees in the workplace : a guide for employers /
  Jennie Kermode.
Description: Philadelphia : Jessica Kingsley Publishers, [2017]
Identifiers: LCCN 2017016306 | ISBN 9781785922282 (alk. paper)
Subjects: LCSH: Transgender people--Employment. | Personnel management.
Classification: LCC HD6285 .K47 2017 | DDC 658.30086/7--
dc23 LC record available at https://lccn.loc.gov/2017016306

British Library Cataloguing in Publication Data
A CIP catalogue record for this book is available from the British Library

ISBN 978 1 78592 228 2
eISBN 978 1 78450 544 8

Printed and bound in the United States

Contents

Introduction

Who this book is for

This book is for business owners, managers, supervisors and human resources (HR) personnel. It is designed to help you better understand transgender (trans) people and the issues they are likely to face in the workplace.

Perhaps you have already decided to take on a trans employee. Perhaps one of your existing staff has decided to transition from male to female or from female to male, or has announced that they do not identify with either a male or a female gender. Perhaps you just want to be prepared in case you find yourself dealing with a situation like this in future. As society is changing and increasing numbers of trans people feel able to live openly, this is something more and more people in your position are having to get the hang of. The good news is that it's not as complicated as it might seem. This book sets out to answer your questions and address your concerns. It also contains information that will be useful to people who are working with trans people on a temporary basis, perhaps in consultation on a particular project or because an agency has provided a temp who happens to be trans. It can help if you are doing business with a trans person who works for another company and you want to avoid accidentally causing offence. If you are an ordinary employee with no special status in your company but you want to be a better friend to a trans colleague, this book could help you to better understand what life is like for that person and what kind of challenges the workplace might present.

Finally, this book will be of use to the organisers of employee support organisations like trade unions and guilds, helping them to be more inclusive and provide a better service to their trans members.

How this book can help

This book will take you through the practical day-to-day issues that having a trans person in the workplace can present. It will help you understand what it means to be trans and will answer some of the questions that it would be rude to ask directly. It will clarify your legal responsibilities and explain what you can do to make trans people feel more comfortable, as well as helping you deal with any related conflicts in the workplace or bad reactions from customers. It will also show you how having trans employees can be beneficial to your organisation, giving you fresh insights into how people interact and helping you to develop a more positive and inclusive workplace culture that enhances your reputation.

A note on language

Because this book sets out to challenge assumptions about gender and deals with many situations in which gender is not specified, the singular form *they* is used. The author notes that some people find this word grammatically objectionable but hopes that you, the reader, will be patient with it. It has been around for at least 300 years in common speech and its meaning should be clear.

The nature of the subject matter in this book is such that you may encounter a number of unfamiliar terms, especially if you are dipping in and out of it rather than reading it straight through. There is a glossary at the end of the book to help you check the meaning of these terms.

Chapter 1

Understanding Transgender People

The Basics

What does it mean to be trans?

Transgender (trans) people are people who feel that their gender identity doesn't match the male or female label they were given at birth. They may have been brought up as boys but want to live as women. They may have been brought up as girls but want to live as men. They may not feel that they are either male or female, or they may feel that they are a bit of both.

What is gender identity?

Everybody has a gender identity. If you were raised as a boy and your gender identity is male, or if you were raised as a girl and your gender identity is female, the chances are that you've never really given it much thought, because the way our society is structured means it will always have been straightforward for you to express yourself just as you are. But not every society is like this. Some societies – in the past and even today – have more complex ways of thinking about gender. They recognise that people's sense of themselves doesn't always fit into one of two neat categories, and that even when it does, it might not be the first one other people associate with their body type.

Gender identity usually develops between the ages of three and seven.[1] This is why some people start identifying as trans at a very young age. Other people, however, just feel that something is wrong and don't work out what it is – or don't feel able to admit it to themselves – until a lot later in life.

Trans people are sometimes described as feeling as if they are trapped in the wrong bodies. This can be a bit misleading because most trans people don't hate their bodies, but they may hate the way that parts of their bodies send out the wrong signals about who they are – to other people and to themselves. Being in this situation is a bit like being constantly mistaken for somebody else, or even seeing a stranger when you look in the mirror. It can be disorientating and very distressing, an experience referred to as gender dysphoria. People who have to deal with dysphoria for a long time are at risk of developing depression, anxiety disorders and related health problems. If they can't get help, they face a high risk of suicide.

For some people, gender dysphoria can be reduced to a manageable level by dressing in a different way or spending time with friends who recognise them for who they really are. For others, the only way to deal with it is by undergoing hormone treatment, having surgery or going through a full process of transition (described later in this chapter) to live permanently in a different gender role.

What is a gender role?

Gender roles are the sets of behaviours we associate with being a man or being a woman (or, in some societies, belonging to other gender groups). For example, a man might be expected to have short hair, be muscular, use a traditionally male name and be referred to as *he* or *him*. He will normally be greeted with a handshake or a pat on the arm in circumstances where a woman might be greeted with a hug or a kiss on the cheek.

Different societies make different associations with gender. For instance, in our society long hair is associated with femininity, but the Vikings didn't see it that way. We associate blue with boys and pink with girls, but for the Victorians those colours were the other way around – pink, being a pale form of red, was seen as too strong a colour for girls, with a pale blue being gentler and therefore more appropriate. Most societies associate gentleness with women to some degree because women give birth to children and are more likely to be their main carers in the early years, but in some societies that's taken to an extreme – women in Saudi Arabia are not allowed out of the house without a male relative who can look after them – whilst in others it's recognised that women can be just as fierce as men, as any fan of roller derby can attest. This means it's naive to assume that there's only one natural set of rules for people of each gender to follow.

Trans people generally don't take gender roles to an extreme, though those who do are likely to attract more attention, which can give a misleading impression of the wider population. Doctors used to think that trans women could only be serious about transition if they wore floral-print dresses and high heels, grew their hair and wore a lot of make-up – something that revealed more about what those doctors thought of women than it did about their patients, who would conform to whatever standards were set for them so that they could get treatment. These days, it's understood that trans women might have short hair and wear jeans, go to football matches and drink beer – just like lots of other women. That doesn't mean, however, that they don't feel a need for core elements of their female gender role to be respected – they want to be called *she*, for instance, not as an affectation but because it feels central to who they are.

At their simplest, gender roles are about how we express ourselves and what others expect of us, and how society views these things. We can all perform different gender roles if we choose to – you could probably play somebody of a different gender on stage, for example, if you put your mind to it – but it's much easier simply to do what comes naturally. What comes naturally for trans people is often at odds with what's expected of them based on the sex category they're put into at birth, and this can make life very difficult for them even before they think about transitioning, or even before they know that such things are possible.

Some people argue that if society treated people of different genders more equitably, there would be no trans people. This is unlikely to be the case because some people's bodies would still feel wrong to them, but as a rule trans people are likely to feel less dysphoric in situations where there is less pressure to conform to a strict male or female role. Dysphoria is often at its worst in strictly segregated environments, including some types of workplace.

Some trans people who feel very uncomfortable about their inability to conform to expectations try to make their own transness go away by taking on roles traditionally associated with the sex category they were put into at birth. For instance, a trans woman might become a soldier or an engineer and behave in a macho way to try to hide the way she feels inside. It's possible that some people manage to keep this up throughout their lives – that's something which it's pretty much impossible to collect data on. What we do know is that other such people find that the pressure of dysphoria becomes overwhelming, and eventually break down and have to face who they really are. This means that it's wrong to assume that a trans woman who seems to have a very masculine background, or a trans man who seems to have a very feminine background, is not serious about transition.

If most of what you've heard about trans people comes from newspapers or television talk shows, be prepared to be surprised. The media often exaggerates trans experiences to make them more newsworthy, just as it does with other stories. In addition to this, people who attract media attention tend to be a bit larger than life. Most trans people are just like anybody else once you set aside their experience of gender. They have rent or mortgages to pay, families or pets to look after, hobbies, career ambitions and the same desire to work in an environment that feels emotionally rewarding.

The transition process

There is a popular belief, often supported by the media, that trans people go into an operating theatre one day and undergo an almost magical process, coming out as a different gender: men become women and women become men. In fact, transition is a lengthy and complicated process with many different elements. It is often seen as beginning with the process of coming out – opening up to other people about being trans. This usually happens first with family members or close friends, but in some cases trans people choose to come out at work before doing so in other areas of their lives. This may be because they anticipate the workplace presenting the biggest challenge and they want to get that over with, or it may be because they don't feel able to come out to those close to them but they think their employers and colleagues will be more open-minded and they want to be able to be themselves on at least a part-time basis.

Transition can be roughly broken down into three elements:

- social transition
- hormonal transition
- surgical transition.

It's important to note that not every trans person will go through all of these stages. The importance of each stage will vary from one person to another. Going through one or two of these stages but not others does not mean that an individual is less serious about being trans.

The latter two stages are discussed in depth in Chapter 9. The most important stage for employers to understand is social transition.

Social transition

Social transition is the process of changing presentation and behaviour with the aim of being accepted by society as a member of a different gender from the one assigned at birth – for example, somebody who was brought up as a girl seeking to be recognised and respected as a man. Because this is a two-way process, with the trans person making changes and society making changes to accommodate them, it's the stage at which they need the most support from others, including employers and work colleagues.

Because social transition is usually the first stage of the overall transition process (and may in some cases be the only stage), people beginning it will generally not look very much like what most others expect of people of the gender they want to present themselves as, and they will sometimes make behavioural mistakes, too. Because most of us are used to strict boundaries between how men and women behave and present themselves – often more so than we're consciously aware of – these incongruities can seem absurd, and may sometimes prompt laughter. It's important to remember how tough this is for the person going through this process of change. When they have had time to settle into their new role, they may sometimes look back and laugh at the mistakes they made, but when they're at this vulnerable stage, anything that feels like ridicule can be deeply damaging.

In trying to understand this, it can be helpful to think about what it's like to be a teenager. All of us learn how to fit into our adult gender roles at some point in life, and it's usually between the ages of about 12 and 18. Boys at this stage often make fools of themselves by trying to be macho. Girls may wear too much make-up, dress clumsily and make a display of being flippant. Although they're a little older and wiser, people who transition as adults are essentially going through this same learning process. If they're shown a bit of sympathy and patience, they'll soon adjust. Some trans people report very positive experiences of being supported at this stage by work colleagues who have taken them on boys' nights out or girls' nights out to enjoy a few drinks and impart supposedly secret gendered knowledge.

Real-life experience

In the United Kingdom, anybody wanting to undergo gender confirmation surgery under the National Health Service (NHS) is first required to go through two years of 'real-life experience'. This means that they are required to present themselves full time in the gender role they are transitioning to, at home, at work, in their social lives and out on the streets. The idea behind this is that it will ensure that nobody undergoes surgery unless they're really serious about it and will be able to cope in their new role. Many trans people feel it's inappropriate, however, because it can make them very vulnerable at a stage when it's hard for them to 'pass', making the fact that they're trans very visible to everyone.

One of the requirements of the real-life experience test is that people going through it must be in education, work or training. This presents another barrier for trans people struggling to find employment. It means that people may feel forced to out themselves at work when they are not emotionally ready for it, simply because the thought of having to wait still longer for surgery is too much to bear. It is vital that employers are supportive in this situation.

Because of the real-life experience requirement, it is impossible for most trans people to get surgery as soon as they are ready to come out. This means that it's unreasonable for employers to say, as some have done, that they will only respect a trans person's gender after surgery has taken place.

Non-surgical transition

Not everybody who goes through the transition process has surgery. Some people don't feel that they need it in order to cope with dysphoria, or don't feel that they should have to change their bodies in order to be accepted for who they are. Other people have medical reasons for not undergoing surgery. Still others are stuck on very long waiting lists and don't want to have to wait years before they begin living authentic lives, so choose to transition socially long before surgery is available to them. Because being unable to undergo wanted surgery can be distressing, it's impolite to ask people about whether they have had surgery or why they haven't had it, unless they volunteer the information.

People who transition without surgery are generally just as sure of their gender as people who do have surgery, and, as a rule, should not be treated differently. Later in this book you will find information on how to deal with situations where other employees express discomfort around trans people who have not gone through surgical transition.

Non-transitioning people

Some trans people don't feel able to transition at all, often for family reasons, because they don't feel an elderly relative would understand or because they believe it would lead to the end of a marriage and they have children to consider. People in this situation may still wish to be open about their identity in some contexts, and if the workplace feels safe in this regard, they are likely to be a lot happier and more productive.

Non-transitioning people can still be upset by hostile remarks or cruel jokes made at the expense of trans people, which makes it all the more important not to allow that kind of behaviour in the workplace – you can never assume that nobody will be directly affected by it.

Non-binary people

An increasing number of scientists think that gender doesn't exist as a simple switch, with everybody being either male or female, but that it exists on a spectrum.[2] This can be imagined as a line with a male end and a female end. Most people will be close to one end of the line and will therefore feel male or female (whether or not their bodies seem to match this).[3] Some people, however, are closer to the middle of the line and do not feel that either label describes them very well.

Non-binary people are not simply people who don't have a very strong sense of gender. They may feel dysphoria just like other trans people and find it very upsetting to live in the gender roles they were given at birth. Transitioning to live in the 'opposite' role, however, is not a solution for them and does not make their dysphoria go away. They need to find a way to live that better fits who they are.

The term *non-binary* is used to describe a range of experiences that individuals may think of in different ways. Some people may feel that it's inaccurate to describe them as male or female but that they're closer to one of those than the other, and may mirror this in certain aspects of their presentation or even in their pronoun choice. Some consider themselves to be trans but others don't. Some feel that they are outside of gender altogether. Others find that their experience of gender fluctuates, a process which can occur over months or even during the course of a single day. Whilst this may sound complicated, it's always possible to work out a practical way of managing it in the context of the workplace. The important thing is simply to sit down and talk through what the individual needs. Once you get to know them (or to see them as they really are, if they didn't feel able to be open about their gender when they first joined your organisation), you'll find that their presentation and behaviour begins to feel as straightforward as anyone else's.

In some cases, people come out as non-binary before deciding that they actually want to transition 'all the way' to male or female. Getting to grips with gender when it doesn't fit standard social expectations can be difficult, so nobody should be surprised that it can take people a while to figure out how they want to live in the long term. It should never be assumed that being non-binary is a phase, however. In fact, some people who have transitioned from male to female, or vice versa, later come to feel that identifying as non-binary is a better fit for them.

The first challenge most employers encounter with non-binary people is knowing which pronouns to use for them. In most cases, neither *he* nor *she* will be appropriate. If you're looking for an interim solution, the best choice is to use *they*. Some people feel uncomfortable about this because it's usually associated with plurals and using it for one person feels like bad grammar. Language is constantly changing, however, and singular *they* has in fact been in common use for over three centuries. You'll find it in the dictionary. It's a useful term because even if some people find it a bit odd at first, almost everybody understands what is meant by it.

Because *they* doesn't feel right to everybody, a number of alternatives have developed within Lesbian, Gay, Bisexual, Transgender and Intersex (LGBTI) communities. The most common of these is *zie/zir* (sometimes spelled *xie/xir* but pronounced the same way in either case). This could be used, for example, to say 'I'm looking for Chris. Have you seen zir? Do you know where zie is?' or to reply 'Chris is at zir desk.' Other pronouns (including pronunciation) used in this way are listed in a helpful table in the glossary at the end of this book.

Using unfamiliar pronouns can feel strange at first, but most people get the hang of it quite quickly. Non-binary people understand that it's challenging and most will not object if mistakes are sometimes made as long as it's clear that there's no ill will behind them. If you're unsure what the best pronouns to use for a particular person are, just ask.

Gender-variant people

Sometimes people are categorised by themselves or others as *gender variant*. Like *non-binary* or *transgender* itself, this can be used as a catch-all term for a variety of gender identities that don't fit traditional expectations, but it's also used to describe people who are in the middle ground between cisgender (see below) and transgender people. This includes people who are experimenting with gender to work out what feels comfortable for them. It also includes people who feel generally comfortable with the gender category they were put into at birth, but fail to fit it in one or two ways that make other people uncertain how to relate to them. For instance, somebody classed as female at birth may identify as a woman but feel really uncomfortable about having breasts and want to get rid of them; or somebody classified as male may be happy living as a man but have a strong desire to wear make-up. In cases like this, a small amount of flexibility from an employer, and respect for that difference, can make it much easier for people to feel comfortable at work and concentrate on doing a good job.

Some employers are uncomfortable about cases like this because they feel that rules designed to accommodate transitioning people are being stretched. Others recognise that issues like this are very real for some people, and want to do the right thing, but worry that they can't tell the difference between genuine cases and cases in which people are trying to exploit them. In this situation, an important place to start is by asking yourself how much it really matters how serious the situation is, or even whether or not it's real. If a rule works perfectly well for female employees, for example, will it really make much difference to the functioning of the business if it's extended to male ones? If an employee is experimenting with changes of gender presentation in a way that may or may not be permanent, does it hurt to ask others to treat them with respect as they do so?

If an employee is merely pretending to be gender variant to get attention, they will usually get bored and desist before long. In fact, one of the best ways to deal with mischief-making of this sort is to treat it matter-of-factly and without any fuss – which is also the best way to respond when gender variance is real.

Cisgender people

Because trans people are not the only people who have a sense of gender, the term *cisgender* was invented. It describes people whose experience of gender matches what most people would expect based on the gender they were classed as at birth. The prefix *cis-* comes from Latin and means *the same* or *on the same side*, whereas *trans* means *in-between* or *crossing over*. Using the term *cisgender* clarifies that trans people are not unusual in feeling that gender is a significant aspect of who they are or how they fit into society. The emergence of the term *cisgender* is similar to the emergence of the term *heterosexual* in the 1890s. Before then, people were either classed as being homosexual or being normal, because to be homosexual was seen as aberrant rather than just different.

Some people object to the term *cisgender* and consider it derogatory, but an increasing number of people are using it to describe themselves. This is especially true of the younger generation. It can be shortened to *cis*, hence *cis man*, *cis woman* or *cis people*.

If you feel that using the term *cisgender* or *cis* will offend your employees, an alternative approach is to use the term *non-transgender* or *non-trans*. This isn't ideal, in that it still marks out being trans, rather than simply having a gender, as the significant factor, but it's better than the default assumption that trans people exist in contrast to normal people. It helps to create parity between trans people and people with a different relationship to their birth gender categories.

Intersex people

One group of people who don't quite seem to fit these definitions are intersex people, and as a result there can be quite a bit of confusion about them. Intersex people do not fall under the 'transgender umbrella' as a group, though some individual intersex people identify as trans and some laws designed to help trans people also apply to intersex people.

Intersex people can be roughly defined as those individuals whose bodies don't fit the standard expectation of what a male body or a female body is like. Some intersex people have different chromosomes – not the familiar XX or XY – whilst others have hormone levels, genitals, secondary sexual characteristics (breasts, body hair, etc.) or internal reproductive anatomy that challenges expectations. Most of these variations don't cause health problems, though intersex people may have been put through surgical procedures when very young in order to make them look more typical – something that *can* cause health problems and that a lot of intersex adults object to.

If they are diagnosed as intersex at birth, people like this are usually given a gender classification on the basis of what doctors think they look most like or are most likely to identify as. More often than with non-intersex births, this decision is wrong, and this leads to some intersex people later going through procedures similar to those that transitioning trans people go through, in order to go some way towards setting things right.

Most intersex people have male or female gender identities, in line with the general population. Some are non-binary and some simply choose to identify a non-binary type gender as intersex, since they feel it matches their bodies. Intersex people may define themselves as cisgender or transgender, or may feel that they exist outside that system of classification.

Many intersex people object to being seen as the same as, or similar to, trans people. This may be because they have gone through experiences that can be highly traumatic and that trans people don't share, or it may be because they feel that trans people have more options than they do about medical interventions and whether or not to live openly. They often experience similar forms of discrimination, however, especially if they have very visible mixed gender physical characteristics, which may lead to them being mistaken for trans people. Much of the advice given to employers in this book can also be applied to working with intersex employees.

Trans people and sexual orientation

Some people find the difference between gender and sexual orientation difficult to understand. The simplest way to think of it is this: *sexual orientation* is about who you're *attracted to* and *gender* is about who you *are*. In fact, being trans has nothing to do with sexual orientation. Trans people can be straight, gay or bisexual, like anybody else. Non-binary people, who find these terms don't fit them very well, are more likely to define their sexuality in terms of who they're attracted to. They may say that they're gynophilic (attracted to women), androphilic (attracted to men), or omnisexual or pansexual, both of which mean that a person has the capacity to be attracted to people of any gender, including non-binary people. Of course, being omnisexual or pansexual doesn't mean that a person is attracted to everybody they meet, any more than being heterosexual means a woman is attracted to every man she meets.

Some of the earliest modern theories about trans people revolved around the idea that they were people who were so ashamed of being gay that they wanted to change sex so that they would be straight. These ideas have been widely discredited – some trans people are openly and happily living as gay people before they transition and some people are seen as gay only after they transition (because, for example, they are moving from a male role to a female one and are consistently attracted to women throughout). Occasionally trans people report that their sexual orientation changes when they transition, but this seems to be rare.

The fact that many organisations cater to lesbian, gay, bisexual *and* transgender people, and some treat them as if their circumstances were identical, is partly as a result of that historical confusion (on the part of academics, not usually trans people themselves) and partly as a result of the fact that these groups face similar types of prejudice and discrimination. Working together has made it easier for them to lobby for equality and for legislative and social changes that can help to get rid of prejudice and discrimination. In the workplace, it means that if there are only one or two trans people then they can potentially be part of a group with lesbian, gay or bisexual people who will understand some of the problems they face and can provide support.

The downsides of LGBT people working together are two-fold. First, employers and others in positions of influence sometimes take a one-size-fits-all approach to everyone covered by this acronym, with trans people often being the ones who, as a result, get left without effective support. Second, it adds to ongoing confusion about sexual orientation and gender identity. It's not uncommon for people to talk about 'transgender people' and 'straight people' as if trans people can't be straight; or for surveys to ask people if they are lesbian, gay, bisexual or transgender and only allow them to tick one box, as if trans people don't have any kind of sexual orientation. As an employer, you should be careful to avoid making mistakes like this.

Common problems trans people face

The first report of the House of Commons Women and Equalities Committee Inquiry into Transgender Equality,[4] published in 2016, found significant problems facing trans people in education, health, the prisons and probation services, and the media. It noted that discrimination is a daily fact of life for trans people, and described some of the reports submitted to it in evidence as 'harrowing'. Citing academic work by the Sussex Hate Crime Project at the University of Sussex, it noted that hate crime can have far-reaching effects, causing fear, anxiety and anger, and producing high levels of psychological trauma in victims. Despite this, hate crime is considered to be massively under-reported, and the report cited Professor Neil Chakraborti's estimate that only 2–3 per cent of incidents are successfully prosecuted.

Trans people are also more likely to suffer from social isolation.[5] Family rejection is becoming less common but is still a serious problem for many, as is losing friends when coming out. They may find themselves unwelcome in community facilities and places of worship. Harassment from neighbours makes some afraid to leave their homes, so they go out only when they have to in order to work, shop or access essential services.

The degree to which trans people experience these problems depends to an extent on how obvious their transness is to others. Trans men may be, on average, shorter than other men, but other than this they don't look unusual after a year or two of hormone treatment, so they're more likely to escape problems. Trans women are more likely to stand out. Any trans person can have problems once word gets around that they are trans, however, and some feel that they shouldn't hide it because they don't want people to think it's something to be ashamed of. Being openly trans in all areas of life can put individuals at increased risk but is likely to make trans people overall safer, because it means that people get used to them.

Given these issues, trans people may be more wary than the average person and more alert to possible hostility, which leads some people to assume they're being oversensitive. In reality, this reaction is a reasonable one and doesn't mean that they're likely to be nervous or averse to risk-taking more generally. Once they know that the people around them can be trusted, they are likely to relax and behave just like anyone else. This is one of the reasons why it's important to make the workplace a welcoming environment, free from prejudice and discrimination. It's something that will allow visitors as well as employees to feel at ease.

One of the challenges this brings up is recognising prejudice. Most people can recognise physical bullying, name-calling and so on, but it's hard to break out of habits we might never have thought about, or to anticipate what might be upsetting to somebody whose situation we struggle to identify with. Whilst most trans people feel uncomfortable if all their colleagues start being hyper-sensitive in an effort to avoid offence, it's important that they have a good enough relationship with the boss, a manager or somebody in HR to be able to point out when they feel they are facing prejudice. If they confront you about your behaviour, don't get defensive. It doesn't mean you're being accused of being a bad person – you might have been doing something by accident. If that doesn't seem to be the case, take some time to think about it. There might very well be something they are seeing clearly but which is hard for you to spot because you're struggling to put yourself in their position.

Taking the time to think through the way prejudice against trans people might manifest in the workplace can also help you to spot areas where you might unintentionally be treating women in a prejudiced way, or allowing employees to do so. Some of the problems encountered by women and trans people are very similar – for instance, having their ideas taken less seriously than those of non-trans men.

Discrimination in employment

Although gender reassignment is a protected characteristic under the Equality Act (2010),[6] there is still evidence showing that trans people frequently encounter discrimination in employment. Like other forms of discrimination, it can be difficult to quantify and prove. Individual cases often come down to one person's word against another's, and subtler forms of discrimination like excluding trans people from opportunities for promotion can be difficult to detect without the use of big data.

Historically, trans people have been significantly more likely to suffer workplace discrimination than lesbian, gay or bisexual people.[7] A 2012 study[8] found that 40 per cent of trans people felt they had faced discrimination when looking for a job and 31 per cent felt they had been discriminated against at work. There is evidence that this figure has grown since more trans people have entered the workplace, but that may be a temporary issue as other studies suggest that prejudice against members of minority groups goes down as people get to know them. In the long term, working alongside trans people is likely to be one of the most important factors in encouraging other people to accept them in society more generally.

More and more trans people are now reporting that they have positive experiences in the workplace, across a range of industries. Though prejudice is more entrenched in some sectors than others, often the challenges of employing a trans person are fewer than employers expect. As long as you make a few basic adjustments and take quick action against any discrimination within your organisation, you're likely to find that things quickly settle down.

How common are trans people?

How likely is it that you will have dealings with one or more trans people at some point in your career? In the early 2000s, estimates put the number of trans people in the United Kingdom at approximately 500,000 – about the size of the population of Sheffield. Those figures, however, focused only on people who felt the need to go through binary transitions with medical help, thereby excluding most non-surgical transitioners, non-transitioning people and non-binary people. They were also collected during a period when public awareness of trans people was much more limited, many trans people themselves could not put a name to their feelings, and many felt the need to keep quiet because of the great stigma associated with being trans.

As society has become more open about these issues, the number of people accessing support services for trans people has almost doubled, as has the number of people formally referred to gender-identity clinics. It used to be thought that there were far more trans women out there than trans men, but now the numbers are about even. People are also transitioning earlier in life, which means that some are able to get it out of the way before they even enter the world of work. Transition is easier and more effective if done earlier in life (especially if puberty blockers can be brought in to prevent the body developing unwanted secondary sexual characteristics at adolescence), so people who transition earlier are likely to fit into their new roles better and have to deal with less hostility. They are also less likely to be traumatised as they won't have had to cope with dysphoria or with pretending to be something they're not for as long as their late-transitioning counterparts.

Research based on equality-monitoring forms suggests that one in every 250 people identifies as non-binary when presented with three gender options on a form. The Equality and Human Rights Commission (EHRC) has estimated that 1.3 per cent of the UK population is trans or gender variant,[9] with around a third of these people being non-binary – that is, around 192,300 people in the United Kingdom, equivalent in number to the population of Northampton.

It is difficult to estimate exactly what the size of the trans population will look like when figures stabilise. What we do know is that one in five people in the United Kingdom now says they know a trans person. The real figure is probably significantly higher, as this will not account for people who are not visibly trans and have not come out to those questioned. A Randstad Workmonitor[10] survey conducted in 2015 found that one in every four people in the United Kingdom has a trans work colleague. In India that figure is one in two, which suggests that the UK figure is likely to rise as more trans people enter the workforce. This is positive news for trans people in general, not just in the workplace, because researchers concur that knowing a trans person makes a person much less likely to be transphobic.

Transphobic prejudice

Prejudice against trans people, commonly called *transphobia*, is widespread in society. Sometimes it's obvious, as in situations where trans people are threatened or attacked in the street, but often it's subtler, and people may not always recognise that they're being prejudiced. We all grow up with certain ways of thinking about other groups of people – attitudes we learn from our parents, from the schools and religious institutions we attend, and from the media. Sometimes these attitudes are sensible – for instance, it's a good thing that we generally trust doctors – but sometimes they're simply incorrect, and can cause harm, so it's important to re-examine them.

If you sometimes find the thought of cross-dressing funny, or if you felt a bit uncomfortable about the subject of this book when you first picked it up, it's probable that you have some transphobic feelings. That's not surprising – it's a product of the culture we live in – but it's something you can change. Learning to engage positively with trans people doesn't mean simply repressing feelings of amusement, hostility or discomfort concerning them. It means examining those feelings, thinking about them in a rational way and trying to understand where they came from. Once most people do this – especially if they're getting to know more about trans people at the same time – those feelings simply go away, because they stop making sense at either a logical or an emotional level.

If you've never had feelings like this, it's still useful to think about them and, if possible, to talk to people who do. This will help you to anticipate situations in which your trans employees might encounter prejudice, and it will help you to reason with prejudiced employees and persuade them to change the way they think about trans people. Examining prejudice is the starting point for interacting respectfully with trans people in the workplace.

Chapter 2

Interacting with Transgender People

Making your position clear

Making trans people feel comfortable in your workplace is not just about fulfilling your legal obligations. It won't just benefit your trans employees – it will directly benefit your business. Research by the Human Rights Campaign Foundation has found that LGBT employees are 20–30 per cent more productive when they don't feel they need to keep secrets about their identity from others in the workplace.[11]

You will never get the chance to show your trans employees that you respect and value them if they leave before transitioning because they assume that coming out is going to be unwelcome. Sadly, the evidence points to this happening on a frequent basis, because people who have encountered a lot of prejudice in wider society can be inclined to assume the worst. This means that it's really important to make your support for trans people clear. There are several ways you can do this:

- Mention trans people specifically in your diversity policy (don't just lump them in with LGBT).

- Make positive statements about inclusivity when promoting your brand.

- Encourage the formation of an LGBT support group that welcomes trans people.

- Put up posters which say that LGBT people are welcome.

- Fly the rainbow flag during LGBT History Month (February).

- Fly the trans flag on Transgender Day of Remembrance (20 November).

- Build relationships with trans-related charities.

- Support your local Pride parade.

Taking actions like this will decrease the risk of you losing valued employees because they don't feel able to come out. It will also broaden the available talent pool when you're recruiting, and it will encourage LGBT people to approach your business as potential customers.

Stella, who works in environmental transport, says:

> Visibility in the workplace is really important. Things like putting the trans flag up for Transgender Day of Remembrance. My managing director wants to make trans much more visible in the workplace. I think people don't realise just how important that is, just to say look, there are trans people out there and some of them work here.

Respectful communication

Many people who want to be respectful to trans people worry that they will get it wrong by using inappropriate language or making incorrect assumptions. If you're working with somebody whom you knew before transition, you might worry about accidentally using the wrong pronouns or an old name. Whilst these things can be upsetting for them, most trans people understand that it's difficult for others to get used to using appropriate language. The most important thing is that they see you making an effort to do better. This chapter outlines some of the things you can do to work towards that.

Using the right language

There are polite and impolite ways to talk to and about trans people. The most important thing is to respect the preferences of the individual concerned, because different people will have different comfort levels and some want to reclaim stigmatised words such as 'tranny'. It's worth bearing in mind that words can send a different message depending on who uses them, so some trans people may feel comfortable with being described in certain ways by other trans people – whom they know are speaking from a position of understanding and sympathy – but will not feel comfortable with other people using the same terms because this is often an indication of hostility. If you are unsure, stick to safe terms and ask individuals what feels right to them.

Be aware that language in this area is evolving fast. New terms may enter common use and older terms may become disparaged. This makes it all the more important to listen to what trans people themselves recommend, and to do so on an ongoing basis. Making contact with local trans support organisations can be a good way to do this without putting pressure on individual employees.

Broadly accepted terms

- *Transgender:* This has two meanings. It is sometimes used as a specific term to refer to people who transition from living as men to living as women, or vice versa. It is also used as an umbrella term for all people whose gender is different from the gender category they were put into when they were born. It should never be used as a noun – nobody is *a transgender* but somebody might be *a transgender person.*

- *Trans:* This is a short form of transgender and is generally the preferred term once the context is clear. It is sometimes written with an asterisk – *trans** – to make clear that it is being used as an umbrella term. This can be a way to emphasise inclusivity.

- *Trans man:* This is the standard term used for a man who began life in a female gender role. You may sometimes see it written as a single word, but it's better to use two words because this emphasises that you don't think of trans men as belonging to a separate category from other men. In this phrasing, *trans* is just an adjective, like *tall* or *shy.*

- *Trans woman:* This is the standard term for a woman who began life in a male gender role.

- *Non-binary person:* This is the most widely accepted umbrella term for people who do not feel they are exclusively male or female. Most such people also use other terms, but it is safest to start with non-binary and then ask the person concerned if they would prefer something else.

- *Transition:* This is the process of somebody moving from one gender role to another. This can be used as a noun or as a verb (e.g. *Sam is transitioning at the moment*).

Problematic terms

- *Transsexual:* This term shares the narrower meaning of *transgender*, referring to people who transition from living as men to living as women, or vice versa. It is rarely used today, however, because of concern that it leads to people confusing gender with sexuality. Use it only for individual trans people who have told you it's what they prefer.

- *Tranny:* This term is sometime used affectionately by gay men and drag queens (who dress up as women for performance purposes but usually have male gender identities). Most trans people, however, find it upsetting because it is strongly associated with pornography and contexts in which people like them are fetishised or demeaned.

- *Shemale:* This term is occasionally used between friends but is widely seen as offensive because it is associated with pornography. It also implies that trans people are partly male and partly female, when in fact the majority are simply male or female and don't want gender roles they have had to fight for to be undermined.

- *Born a man* or *born a woman:* Many trans people point out that this would have been painful for their mothers! It's a crude way of putting things which is also problematic, because most trans people feel they have had consistent experiences of gender throughout life – it is other people who have got it wrong. For instance, a trans man may change his body to look more masculine, but feel that he has always been male inside.

Some people who have transitioned in the past no longer see themselves as transgender because they no longer experience dysphoria, even though they may still encounter prejudice at the hands of other people. In order to include people like this in diversity surveys or similar projects, it can be useful to create categories for *men with a trans background* and *women with a trans background.*

You can find a glossary of terms at the end of this book.

Misgendering

Most trans people have gone through many years of struggle trying to cope in the wrong gender role, and have had to fight to have their real gender recognised. This means that they find it very upsetting to be treated as if they were still in the wrong gender category. Such treatment is known as *misgendering*.

The most common form of misgendering is inappropriate use of language, such as referring to somebody using the wrong pronoun, using the wrong gendered title or, for example, calling a trans man a woman. This can happen accidentally, in which case a prompt apology can remove some of the sting. Sadly, it's also a common form of harassment, and it can be a problem in the workplace if a trans employee is not fully accepted by colleagues. If some employees who are not hostile get it wrong frequently due to lack of effort, it can help to explain to them why it can be distressing.

Misgendering can also take other forms – for instance, separating employees into male and female groups without taking account of a non-binary employee, or asking a trans woman to join the male group in such a situation. In any situation where gender is going to be an issue, employers should take care to ensure that misgendering does not occur.

'Real men' and 'real women'

Sometimes people who do not necessarily have any ill-will towards trans people can cause distress by using terms like 'real man' or 'real woman' in a way that implies that they don't fall into these categories. Whilst a lot of trans people simply want to be recognised as men or women and don't take the concept of realness very seriously, language like this is problematic because it can give the impression that they are not *valid* or *natural* men or women, entrenching discrimination and potentially putting them at risk. As history has often shown, when a group of people are perceived as unnatural, they are more likely to be mistreated.

The concept of realness and unrealness has historically been used to support the marginalisation of a lot of people. Feminists, lesbians and even women with short hair have been told that they are not real women. Gay men, men who are not very muscular and men who prefer to resolve conflict with discussion rather than violence have been told that they are not real men. Often the notion of what is real is focused on a small group of people who have a lot of social advantages. For example, African American men have had to struggle to have their masculinity respected as real.

Some women argue that the experience of growing up as a woman in a sexist world has a powerful impact on personal development and that trans women do not share this. This is true to an extent (in that they are unlikely to have experienced the same pressures as other girls, even if they always understood themselves to be girls), but it's better to acknowledge it in a more constructive way. Instead of thinking about women as trans or real, it helps to think about them as trans or cis, or trans and non-trans, so that the focus is on differences in the life journey rather than differences in the person. After all, people who grow up with major disabilities have a very different life journey from non-disabled people, but we don't (or shouldn't) think of them as less real because of it.

Things to avoid

Although it's a good idea to ask people which terms they prefer, it's always best to do this in an open way rather than by suggesting terms, as the latter approach can cause distress or make people feel pressured into agreeing to things they're not really comfortable with.

It is never appropriate to ask trans people to reveal intimate details about their bodies or their medical histories, any more than it would be with anybody else. If you have a specific concern relating to that person's role in the workplace, ask about capacity rather than directly about their body, and make sure you're not requiring anything of them that you would not require of a non-trans employee.

Many trans people feel awkward about their voices or aspects of their bodies that are hard to change. It's important to be sensitive about this. Although non-trans people often worry about some of the same things – for instance, women who feel they have too much body hair or men who try hard to make their voices sound deeper – these things are likely to be more upsetting for trans people because of their experience of people not recognising or respecting their gender.

Be aware that it's possible to be insulting with compliments, too, if you don't think things through. Sometimes unwitting prejudice shows through this way because we're all more careless when we're being nice. Whilst some people may find comments like 'You look really good, even though you're trans' amusing, others, even if they appreciate the good intentions behind them, will find them stressful. By contrast, somebody simply saying 'You look really good' is not problematic at all.

Inclusiveness in workplace communications

Sometimes the language used in day-to-day communications can inadvertently exclude trans people. Although this may seem trivial, experiencing small problems of this sort all the time can be very wearing. It doesn't take long to get into good habits that help people to feel included. Below are some things to pay attention to:

- Avoid unnecessary gendered terms – for example, don't say 'the men and women in this company' when you could just as easily say 'the people in this company'.

- Avoid contrasting trans people with 'normal' people. Instead of saying 'trans people and everyone else', say 'trans people and cis people' or 'trans and non-trans people'.

- If you are unsure about the title an employee wishes to be referred to by, ask! If you think you might forget, make a note.

- Consider dropping the use of gendered titles altogether in contexts where they're not really necessary.

- Avoid jokes about gender (even if they're about men and women more generally) as they can easily misfire or be misinterpreted.

- If your workplace has a women's group that welcomes trans women, mention that explicitly when writing about it, as trans women may otherwise be uncertain about whether or not others will want them there.

Why language matters

Kit is a trans man who initially came out to his employer as non-binary. He was not well-supported and none of his colleagues used the right pronouns. He says:

I was going home from work at lunch crying and not wanting to go back. I had one good friend who worked there and my friend said to the manager, 'Kit is really unhappy. You have to do something about this.' She called me in for a meeting and the first thing she said was, 'I'm sure nobody is doing any of this intentionally.' It was an immediate silencing tactic... I cried in a couple of meetings, so they wrote me off as too emotional. They eventually said they would enter into the very long process of trying to find someone who would do training. I had an email offering me a temporary job elsewhere and decided, 'That's it, I'm leaving.' They didn't accept my resignation at first. They even tried to get me to come in after having left and get me to advise on trans awareness training.

By letting Kit down so badly, his employer lost an experienced employee and also lost the goodwill of another employee, his friend, who remained supportive throughout the process. The employer put the focus on Kit when it should have been on the employees who were behaving disrespectfully. No assumptions should have been made about the reasons for their behaviour prior to investigation, and the employer should have been alert to the fact that experiencing ongoing disrespect can make any employee emotional. Had Kit chosen to take his employer to court, he may well have been awarded compensation.

Trans people protesting about language issues are often told that they might have bigger things to worry about, but the ongoing experience of being addressed and referred to in inappropriate ways, when it's clear that no effort is being made to get things right, can be very distressing. It sends the message that other people in the workplace either don't respect the fact that the employee is trans, or don't care enough about their well-being to make the effort. This is very different from a situation in which people are making occasional mistakes. Most trans people see the latter as inevitable, especially in the early days after transitioning in the workplace, when colleagues are trying to break with long-established habits.

Dealing with mistakes

If you make a mistake when talking to or about a trans person, what should you do about it? If you're in private, it's usually best to apologise straightaway, but keep it simple and don't make a fuss – in most cases the trans person, reassured that you didn't mean to be rude, would rather just forget about it and continue with the conversation.

Hazel worked in an engineering firm with a very male-dominated culture, and one day received a note from her boss in which the boss came out as trans and explained that she would be leaving her old male identity behind and returning to work, after a break, as a woman. The boss asked Hazel if she could let the rest of the team know. This was the first time Hazel had handled a situation of this type and she decided that it would be best to phone each member of her team directly, rather than trusting to email. She talked the matter through with them individually, allowing them room to express their surprise at a situation that no-one on her team had seen coming.

Hazel knew that the people on her team were good people and wasn't worried that they would react badly, but found that a lot of them were worried about making mistakes, addressing the boss incorrectly or accidentally using the wrong name. She was concerned that if they were hyper-sensitive they would create more discomfort than if they were just being themselves, so encouraged them to relax and just deal with mistakes when they happened, which worked out well for everyone. Lucy, a trans woman who works in aerospace engineering, says:

> If you transition and you go back to work, I've found that people have been really, really embarrassed when they get the gender wrong. I'm actually completely relaxed about it as long as it's accidental.

Equality and fairness

As an employer, you should ensure equality in the workplace by being careful to treat all your employees fairly – but this is not the same thing as treating them equally. This can be a confusing concept. It's easiest to understand by considering examples.

To take a very basic example: if you run a factory in which some people are doing hard physical work whilst other people sit at desks taking orders, it's fair to give the people doing the physical work more breaks. If you restricted the physical workers to the three breaks per shift that you were giving to the desk workers, they would quickly become exhausted, whilst the desk workers would not. Therefore, even though you would be treating them equally, the resulting situation would be unfair.

In most circumstances you will not need to make special adjustments in order to be fair to the trans people in your workplace, but you should always be alert in case situations develop where this is necessary. Because trans people are more likely to face prejudice or discrimination in the workplace than most other employees, you should have monitoring in place to watch out for this so that you can react quickly if a problem develops. For example, if you run a large company and your monitoring reveals that trans people are not getting promoted as often as the average worker, you may need to institute special measures, such as requiring them to be included on shortlists, in order to make the situation fair.

Sometimes you may find that employees complain about having to use 'special' pronouns for non-binary colleagues, or about trans employees getting 'special' consideration in the uniforms they wear. It's important to explain to them that what they think of as special treatment is simply there to make sure that things are fair. In these cases, colleagues already address non-trans employees by pronouns they're comfortable with, and they get to wear appropriate uniforms, so all the 'special' treatment is doing is making sure that their trans colleagues have the same experience.

Developing a trans-inclusive equality and diversity policy

Having an equality and diversity policy is not only a legal requirement, it's key to ensuring that you can identify problems with prejudice and discrimination that may occur within your workplace. Many otherwise good equality and diversity policies fall down when it comes to trans people, probably due to poor knowledge. How can you make sure yours doesn't? The following simple steps should help:

- Consult stakeholders. If there are no trans people within your organisation, contact a trans or LGBT group for advice. Stonewall, which used to campaign for the rights of gay, lesbian and bisexual people but now includes trans people as well, has a long history of supporting employers in this area. You may also be able to find trans people in your local area who are happy to give advice as you begin developing your policy, and to check it afterwards to make sure there are no errors. If all else fails, the Internet can be a helpful tool for connecting with trans people, and can help you to identify individuals who have experience working in your sector.

- Read existing policies. There are a lot of publicly available policies out there, including policies created by companies with a good reputation for their handling of trans issues. Yours doesn't need to be exactly the same – it should reflect the specific needs of your workplace and your company ethos – but you can benefit from drawing on other people's good ideas. As well as looking at company policies, you can look at those used by public institutions such as the NHS or your local police service.

- Set out your aims. These should not be too detailed. They will form the backbone of your policy and help you to make sure that what follows is cohesive. You will be able to check the rest of the policy against them to make sure that every element is contributing effectively to the whole. They will help you to develop your policy statement. At this stage you won't need to be specific about trans inclusion, but you should make sure not to do anything exclusionary – for example, by using language that assumes everybody working for your company will be male or female.

- Set out your principles. This is the meat of the policy. A good approach is to keep a list of each of the equality strands covered by the Equality Act beside you, making marks next to them as you go in order to make sure they're all adequately covered. You can also use this approach to make sure you use a balanced set of examples. Make sure that, as in the Act, trans people are mentioned specifically and are not simply lumped into LGBT, as the kinds of discrimination trans people face can be quite different from those faced by lesbian, gay and bisexual people.

- Sum up your aims in regard to equality and diversity. This can be a good place to include a simple mission statement.

- Provide details of who is responsible for developing and enforcing the policy and how they can be contacted.

Chapter 3

Key Employer Responsibilities

The United Nations (UN) Guiding Principles on Business and Human Rights

Although they do not create any direct obligations for businesses, the UN *Guiding Principles on Business and Human Rights*[12] are considered the international gold standard in relation to how businesses interact with their employees. They were designed as a framework for establishing how well governments are succeeding in getting businesses to meet their human rights obligations, and they have the support of the UK government. They provide a useful benchmark for employers who want to make sure they're getting things right, and they are part of the reason why businesses with a good record on human rights have a better chance of securing government contracts.

The UN guiding principles are based on the idea that businesses must *respect* and *protect* their employees' human rights, and provide *remedy* where those rights have been breached. They ask states to do the following:

- Enforce laws that require business enterprises to respect human rights, and assess the adequacy of those laws at reasonable intervals.

- Ensure that other laws concerning businesses don't constrain their respect for human rights.

- Provide adequate guidance to businesses on how to show respect for human rights in all their activities.

- Encourage businesses to identify, record and communicate the way their activities impact on human rights.

When it comes to trans people in the workplace, there are three key ways you can make sure your business is acting in accordance with these principles:

- Identify the most serious risks to the human rights of trans employees (most commonly, these will be issues relating to physical safety, privacy and equal treatment in the workplace) and put in place procedures to systematically address these risks. This should be done in partnership with trans people themselves and should include the development of appropriate remedies to be applied if things go wrong.

- Develop the culture and practices of the business so that trans people's rights are fully acknowledged and respected, and seek to increase knowledge about them among both management and employees.

- Conduct regular equality audits that monitor the situation of trans people in the workplace, and track progress in addressing problems and risks.

This information can contribute to the production of equality reports that have the potential to strengthen the reputation of the business and help it win the respect of government and equality organisations.

Observing these principles provides a helpful template for structuring your overall policy concerning trans employees, and helps you to ensure that the various issues discussed in this book can be brought together and managed as part of a cohesive, human rights-based approach.

Trans people and the law

As an employer, you have certain obligations to trans people under the law. It's important to understand these even if you don't have any trans employees that you know of at present, because they start to apply the moment you meet somebody who is trans, and they can apply to interactions with customers or people in other companies as well as your own staff.

Your legal responsibilities will differ depending on where your business is based, as there are different laws affecting trans people in the legal system of England and Wales, the legal system of Scotland, and the legal system of Northern Ireland. The long-term trend is towards increasing the protections trans people are given under the law, so following the strictest of these laws where they apply directly to your own practice can get you into good habits that will ensure you are prepared for any changes.

The Equality Act (2010)

In England, Scotland and Wales, the most important piece of legislation you need to be familiar with is the Equality Act (2010).[13] This identifies nine protected characteristics:

- age
- disability
- gender reassignment
- marriage and civil partnership
- pregnancy and maternity
- race
- religion
- sex
- sexual orientation.

It's important to note that many people fall into more than one of these categories. For example, a trans woman might also have a disability or face hostility because of the colour of her skin. This means that it's useful to try to think about this list holistically.

The characteristic directly relevant to trans people in the Equality Act is *gender reassignment*. This is described as follows:[14]

> (1) A person has the protected characteristic of gender reassignment if the person is proposing to undergo, is undergoing or has undergone a process (or part of a process) for the purpose of reassigning the person's sex by changing physiological or other attributes of sex.

(2) A reference to a transsexual person is a reference to a person who has the protected characteristic of gender reassignment.

(3) In relation to the protected characteristic of gender reassignment—

(a) a reference to a person who has a particular protected characteristic is a reference to a transsexual person;

(b) a reference to persons who share a protected characteristic is a reference to transsexual persons.

Although this is ostensibly a very narrow definition and the guidelines in the *Employment Statutory Code of Practice*[15] say that it only applies to people who have at some point proposed to undergo gender reassignment (implying a binary transition process), the legal system has shown a tendency to interpret it quite broadly, more in line with general social perceptions of what it means to be trans, which have changed since this law was made. In some cases, non-binary people have been able to use the Act, and the term *process* in clause (1) has been interpreted as including counselling, so the provisions of the Act are not limited to people whose transitions involve surgery or hormones.

The Equality Act forbids direct discrimination (where because a person is trans they are treated less favourably than someone who is not); indirect discrimination (where, for example, toilet breaks are limited to five minutes and no special provision is made for trans people who need longer because of the after-effects of recent surgery); harassment; and victimisation. There is also a special clause relating to trans people that makes it illegal to treat a person who needs time off work due to transition less favourably than a person who needs time off work for a different health-related reason.

There is also a clause in the Act that makes it illegal to discriminate against or harass a person because they are associated with a person who is intending to undergo, is undergoing, or has undergone gender reassignment. This means, for example, that an employer cannot treat an individual less favourably because they have a trans spouse.

Employers will also be in breach of the law if they arrange for trans people to be discriminated against on their behalf – for example if they ask a recruitment agency not to refer any trans candidates to them.

The provisions of the Equality Act apply to employees and contract workers (as well as other people the company may interact with, such as customers). An individual does not need to have told their employer that they are trans in order to be protected by the Act.

The Equality Act only applies to trans people who are serious about their gender. It cannot be used by employees who want to get away with dressing up for a joke, so employers do not need to worry that it will be abused. If another employee responds to a trans employee coming out by ridiculing the situation and saying they will wear whatever they like, they can be disciplined as normal without fear of penalty under this law.

There are a limited number of exceptions to the way the Equality Act affects employers: it is possible to discriminate against transgender people on the basis of genuine occupational requirements. These form a legally specific category, however, and are subject to strict definitions.

A religious organisation can refuse to employ a trans person if it can show that:

- the employment is 'for the purposes of an organised religion' [16]

- the requirement that the employee not be trans is consistent with the doctrines of the religion *or*

- the employee being trans would conflict with the religious convictions of a significant number of followers of the religion.

Employers who provide communal accommodation for their employees are permitted to exclude trans people from that accommodation, but may only do so if it is a proportionate means of achieving a legitimate aim. This should be assessed on a case-by-case basis. If, for example, a trans woman wants to use communal accommodation provided for women and none of the other women using the accommodation object to this, it's unlikely that the employer would be able to justify that exclusion in a court.

The Public Sector Equality Duty

Under the provisions of the Equality Act, all public sector employers in England, Scotland and Wales have a statutory duty to have due regard to the importance of eliminating discrimination, harassment and victimisation. They are also obliged to have regard to advancing equality of opportunity and fostering good relations between people who have particular protected characteristics and people who do not.

The public sector Equality Duty[17] requires public sector bodies with 150 or more employees to collect and publish information on employees with protected characteristics. See Chapter 5 for details of how to manage such information without breaching the Data Protection Act or putting confidentiality at risk.

There is some flexibility regarding the precise information to be collected, which allows employers to consider the different issues likely to be relevant in their specific organisations. In general, though, it should include the following:

- information on the make-up of the workforce, making it possible to see at a glance what proportion of employees have particular protected characteristics

- information on recruitment and retention rates for employees with each protected characteristic

- information on any inequality found in remuneration, promotion or training opportunities that relates to protected characteristics

- information on disciplinary issues, mapped against protected characteristics

- information on employee complaints, mapped against protected characteristics.

All public sector employers are required to publish information on people with protected characteristics who are affected by their organisation's policies and practices, which could include, for example, service-users or employees of a company with which the organisation is partnering.

It's also important to recognise what the public sector Equality Duty does not require:

- Employers do not have to ask every employee for details of their protected characteristics (though they may wish to do so for broader equality monitoring purposes, and should consider doing so anonymously to get more accurate results).

- Employers do not have to ask service-users about their protected characteristics, and should never do so unless it is the only means by which they can obtain demographic information necessary for their organisations to function effectively.

- Employees are not obliged to provide information on protected characteristics if they prefer not to.

Public bodies must also publish at least one measurable equality objective every four years, and report on any progress they have made towards it. This could include, for example, increasing the number of trans people it employs by a specific amount. Larger organisations are generally expected to commit to more equality objectives than smaller ones. It's useful to consult with employees and to take account of data on equality in employment more generally when determining what these objectives should be.

Information relating to the public sector Equality Duty does not need to be published separately but can be included in, for example, the organisation's Annual Report. It must, however, be easy to access from both inside and outside the organisation. Public bodies that are doing well on equality may wish to publish their information in a separate Equality Report in order to emphasise this and use it to promote their brand.

Sex Discrimination Regulations (Northern Ireland [NI]) (1999)[18]

The Sex Discrimination Regulations state that it is not permissible to discriminate in employment on the grounds that a person intends to undergo gender reassignment, is undergoing gender reassignment or has undergone gender reassignment. The Sex Discrimination (NI)[19] order also protects trans people from harassment and from discrimination relating to any plans they have to go through a medical transition process; so, for example, it is unlawful to turn somebody down for a job because they are going to need time off for surgery.

The Gender Recognition Act (2004)[20]

The Gender Recognition Act enables trans people who want to be legally recognised as members of the sex they have transitioned to, to apply for a Gender Recognition Certificate (sometimes abbreviated to GRC). With this certificate, they can apply for an amended birth certificate (recognising that their gender was misidentified when they were born), marry or form a civil partnership in their new gender role, and apply to receive a pension in accordance with that role (there are ongoing legal battles over whether or not such pensions will be awarded).

Not every trans person has, or will obtain, a Gender Recognition Certificate. In Northern Ireland, married trans people are first obliged to divorce, and civilly partnered trans people are required to dissolve their partnerships. Some people feel that this is against their principles or don't want to do it because of the distress it would cause to their loved ones. They may also hesitate because it can have a knock-on impact on pension entitlements.

Elsewhere in the United Kingdom, divorce is not a requirement but a married trans person and their spouse have to fill out a statutory declaration form to confirm that they agree to stay together, and the spouse has the option of using the request for gender transition as grounds for divorce. If one or both spouses wish(es) to end the marriage, or if the statutory declaration is not filled out, the trans person will receive an Interim Gender Recognition Certificate. In Scotland, this can (with the permission of the Sheriff court) be immediately converted into a full certificate (effectively meaning that the declaration requirement is moot). In England and Wales it can only be converted into a full certificate after a divorce has been finalised.

Civilly partnered people living in England, Scotland or Wales have the option of either dissolving their civil partnerships or converting them into marriages in order to be eligible for Gender Recognition Certificates.

There is, at the time of writing, no Gender Recognition Certificate system to acknowledge the gender of non-binary people in the United Kingdom. Intersex people are not allowed to use the Gender Recognition Certificate process even if they have changed the gender role in which they live from the one assigned to them when they were children.

Some trans people simply feel that it is not the business of the state to give them permission to be themselves, and do not use the Gender Recognition Certificate process for this reason. Others worry that having a certificate can mark them out as trans in government records and could therefore make them vulnerable if a government hostile to trans people came into power. They cite the way that registration of ethnic status has been used to single people out for discrimination in some parts of the world. This can be a particular issue for people from countries with a recent record of such behaviour.

Employers should not assume that a trans person without a Gender Recognition Certificate is less serious about being trans or about the process of transition. The *Employment Statutory Code of Practice*[21] stresses that trans employees should not be routinely asked to show Gender Recognition Certificates in order to prove their legal status because that represents an intrusion into their privacy.

It is illegal to for an employer to disclose that an employee has received a Gender Recognition Certificate without that person's explicit permission. Doing so, or disclosing that a person who has such a certificate is trans (again, without permission) could result in a fine. If you have been asked by a trans employee to reveal that they are trans (e.g. because they want other staff members to know but don't want to have to discuss it with them personally), it's a good idea to get permission in writing.

When a trans person has been able to obtain an amended birth certificate under this system, it can sometimes make it easier for an employer to update records. This is because it makes it clear to other agencies that they have an obligation to cooperate. It means that the employer can protect the employee's privacy by saying simply that there is an error in the records, which can be proven without the need to reveal the Gender Recognition Certificate itself.

Hate crime laws

Hate crime laws apply to acts that are already criminal – such as assault or threatening behaviour – when those acts are exacerbated by prejudice relating to specific protected characteristics. They differ in different parts of the United Kingdom.

Hate crime laws are not intended to send the message that some people deserve more protection than others. Rather, they are intended to communicate that prejudice itself is wrong and can be an aggravating factor in a crime. Crimes motivated by prejudice don't just harm their immediate targets but also intimidate other people with the same characteristics. An attack on a trans person, for example, can make other trans people living in the same area afraid to go out if it's clear that the assailant had a transphobic motive. Such crimes don't always happen face to face – they might take the form of damage to property with graffiti that makes the motive clear, or they could involve threats made over the Internet.

Hate crimes can be an issue for employers if they occur within the workplace, whether they are perpetrated by another employee, a customer or a visitor (such as a delivery driver employed by a supplier).

In England and Wales, a crime is a hate crime if the person committing it is motivated by prejudice against transgender identity. It doesn't matter who the target is – what matters is what the perpetrator believes. This means that non-binary people as well as trans men and trans women are protected by the law. It also means that a non-trans person who is mistakenly thought to be trans is protected by the law.

In addition to this, a crime is a hate crime if it takes place because of the target's association with a person who has a protected characteristic. This means that if you are threatened by somebody who says they don't like you having trans employees, you could be the victim of a hate crime. If one of your employees is harassed because they have a trans colleague, that harassment could be a hate crime.

Because a lot of people don't understand the difference between gender and sexual orientation, trans people are often victims of homophobic hate crimes. It's important to be able to distinguish the type of prejudice involved if a case goes to court.

Hate crimes are usually identified as such for one of three reasons:

- The language used by the perpetrator when the crime is being committed – this makes it important to pay attention and make notes on this as soon as possible.

- Prejudice the perpetrator has displayed previously that can be connected to the incident – for example, if they told friends that they were going to go and beat up a trans person.

- Prejudice raised by the perpetrator when talking about what they have done – whether they are boasting to friends or confessing to the police.

In Scotland, the definition of transgender identity used in hate crime law is very expansive, explicitly covering trans men, trans women and non-binary people. It also extends to cover intersex people. People who are mistaken for trans people, and people who are targeted because of their association with trans people, can be victims of hate crimes just as they can in England and Wales. It's possible to prosecute a crime as a hate crime on the basis of any two protected characteristics, so if it's not clear whether someone was targeted because they were recognised as trans or because they were assumed to be gay, lesbian or bisexual, a prosecution can still be successful.

In Northern Ireland, being transgender has only recently been included as a protected characteristic in hate crime law. It is limited to offences committed against people who are themselves trans, are cross-dressers, or are believed by the perpetrator to fall into one of these groups.

Anybody can report a hate crime. Because it may result in witnesses having to go to court, it's best to discuss it with the person who was targeted first, to see what they want to do. If one of your employees has been targeted and thinks it should be reported but doesn't feel up to dealing with the police straightaway, you can step in to make the initial report, even if you didn't witness the incident directly.

You can find further information on dealing with hate crimes in Chapters 6 and 8.

The Companies Act

Under the provisions of the Companies Act 2006 (as amended in 2016), if you are a public interest company with over 500 employees, you should disclose information about all equality work 'to the extent necessary for an understanding of the development, performance or position of the company's business'.[22] In other words, you should explain your policy and its outcomes, your approach to risk management and any business relationships that you anticipate could have adverse impacts. This legislation was developed to incorporate the European Union (EU) Non-Financial Reporting Directive 2014,[23] so it helps to ensure a consistent approach across the continent and makes it easier for you to discuss equality practice with potential international trading partners. This is likely to remain the case after Brexit.

Trans people and pension schemes

At present, there are differences in when people can start receiving their state pensions based on what gender they are. These differences are being phased out but, at the time of writing, still affect some people.

For trans people, state pensions are awarded on the basis of the gender recorded on the birth certificate unless they have a Gender Recognition Certificate, in which case that takes precedence. This means that people who were classed as male at birth but are now legally recognised as female may get their pensions earlier as a result; by contrast, people who were classed as female but are now legally recognised as men may have to wait longer to receive their pensions.

Although the Marriage (Same Sex Couples) Act 2013[25] ensures that the partners of people who obtain legal gender recognition after transitioning in England and Wales are still entitled to receive survivor benefits offered by their occupational pension schemes, and similar legislation exists in Scotland, there can be complications or delays if the pension provider has not been informed of the transition. If one of your employees is planning to transition, you should remind them to contact the pension provider for your workplace straightaway if they receive a Gender Recognition Certificate.

Prior to 2014, people in marriages or civil partnerships had to end them before they were allowed to obtain Gender Recognition Certificates. Some people felt that they had no choice but to do this even though their relationships were happy ones and they continued to live with their former spouses or civil partners. Different pension scheme providers take different approaches to people in this situation. They may or may not continue to offer survivor benefits to the former spouse or civil partner. If they do so, they may or may not offer the full amount that would be available if the divorce or dissolution had not occurred. If the couple has since contracted a new marriage or civil partnership, they may or may not pay a level of benefit that takes the earlier period of union into account. Trans people in this situation should contact the company occupational pension provider for advice. As an employer, issues like this are among the factors you may wish to take into account when choosing a pension provider for your organisation.

If your pension provider requires information on gender, trans employees who do not have Gender Recognition Certificates will need to contact them to confirm their officially recognised gender. You should make sure that contact details for the pension provider are easy to access without any difficult questions being asked, so that any trans employees who have chosen not to come out to you are able to handle this requirement without feeling forced to do so.

If you have bought an annuity or insurance policy for an employee based on their contributions to a contracted-out pension scheme, and that employee has subsequently transitioned, the annuity or insurance policy will not be affected, even if its provisions were based in part on gender.

Helping an employee who comes out as trans

No matter how many times somebody has done it before, coming out as trans is always a nerve-racking experience. People doing it know that they may be met with disbelief, mockery, rejection or outright hostility. Many have already been through negative experiences when coming out to other people. Some approach it pragmatically but others do it only when they feel they have no choice, and in a work context they may be afraid that they are putting their jobs on the line by doing so.

Although there is no way to make coming out painless, you can help by having a clear, positively asserted anti-discrimination policy that mentions trans people directly. Some organisations do this as a box-ticking exercise, so you will need to work a bit harder to show that you're committed to it. This could be something as simple as having a poster about it in the workplace, mentioning it in speeches or flying a rainbow flag in support of your local Pride parade. All these things will increase the confidence of your trans employees and make it more likely that they will come out to you quickly, minimising stress and helping you to build positive connections.

When an employee comes out as trans, you have two jobs. The first is to show that you personally are ready to support them. The second is to work out how best to manage the situation in the workplace. There may be no need for other people to know at all. If someone is planning to transition, however, changes will become apparent to other people, and it is usually best to be open with them about what is happening.

Remember that whether or not to come out to other people, and when to do it, is the trans person's decision. You can discuss the practicalities but you should never second-guess that decision or tell people they are trans without explicit permission.

Trade unions

Most trade unions now have LGBT support groups and some have trans-specific support groups. Many also have officers who are specially trained in supporting trans members. If your employee is a member of a trade union, it's often a good idea to ask if they want to invite such a representative to join them in a meeting about how you can best accommodate their needs as a trans person in your workplace. This can be as helpful to you as it is to them, because it gives you instant access to advice on how to proceed, and makes it easy for you to ask questions about areas where neither you nor your employee may be sure of the best course of action. An experienced union representative of this type can often provide detailed examples of how these challenges are being met elsewhere in your industry.

Having a good relationship with a union representative like this can also be helpful if, further down the line, you find that conflict arises between your employees because of how others respond to working with a trans person. Because they are perceived as more neutral than you, and because most employees start from the assumption that the union is on their side, they can sometimes achieve a successful resolution in situations where you are unable to.

Helping an employee who wants to transition

When an employee approaches you with plans to transition, what can you do to help? What sort of issues are likely to arise, and how can you prepare?

People commonly approach transition in one of two different ways. A few decide to take the bull by the horns, just turning up one day in different clothes, using a different name, and aiming to deal with everything at once. Sometimes this bold approach is very effective in deterring criticism but it requires a lot of courage and it can go wrong if people react badly. This is perhaps why most trans people start by changing little things, such as the way they style their hair, and get people used to thinking of them as a bit androgynous before they take bigger steps like changing their names.

Although employers can sometimes help, if asked, to work out which approach is likely to be best in their particular workplaces, the decision about how to begin transition and when belongs solely to the trans person. Employers can help by preparing for certain steps in advance. For example, if they know which day a change of name is going to take place on, they can alter badges, signs and databases in preparation for it. They can set aside time for a short announcement to be made, they can make an announcement on the trans person's behalf (with permission), or they can take a subtler approach, telling key staff one at a time or sending round an email message. Because people who are just coming out can find it exhausting answering colleagues' questions, it can be helpful if a member of staff who understands the key issues is available to talk to any other employees who feel they need to know more.

When Sile decided to come out as a trans woman at work, she spoke to her HR department and the Equalities Officer at her union, Prospect. When her doctor (GP) recommended that she begin a medical transition process, they got together and drew up a plan to ensure that things could be managed as smoothly as possible. They set a date by which her new name and details would be uploaded into the system at the library where she worked. From that date, she would also present fully as female and start using female facilities. She subsequently met with her line manager and the senior cataloguer at the library, and they agreed to inform her colleagues in small groups over the coming days and then inform the other managers in the building where she works. She said afterwards:

> This has now been done and everyone is acquainted with my situation, many also giving me verbal and email support. My employer is LGBT-friendly and will continue to review its policies to see what can be improved.

Making a plan like this is the easiest way to ensure that things run smoothly and that different tasks (such as updating records and informing people) can be coordinated. Plans should be subject to frequent review, however, and should incorporate enough flexibility to make it possible to deal with unexpected challenges (such as colleagues reacting badly or databases resetting themselves).

People who are just beginning the transition process are likely to be feeling vulnerable and can easily become targets for harassment. Employers should pay extra attention to this risk, and can do a lot to minimise it by taking a matter-of-fact approach to the transition themselves. You will find advice in Chapter 6 on what to do if harassment does occur.

People who are just beginning to transition may have difficulty with documentation in various aspects of their lives because it can take quite a while to get everything changed. Employers can help by supplying appropriate work-related documentation as promptly as possible.

Over half of people who have transitioned at work say they feel that their performance has improved as a result. They generally put this down to increased confidence and decreased anxiety, and say that they feel able to concentrate better when they're not also having to make an effort to conform to ill-fitting gender roles. The small number who feel that their performance has got worse report that they have had poor or non-existent support from management, and are also likely to have suffered ongoing harassment from colleagues.

Sile says:

> The support I've received so far has been absolutely amazing; it has made a big difference. It's like having a weight lifted from me. I do feel that transitioning will help me in my work, being able to concentrate fully on what I'm required to do.

Ensuring your responsibilities are met

To make sure you have fully understood and taken account of the issues raised in this section, ask yourself the following questions:

- Would a trans person in your organisation know who to go to in order to get help? Is a back-up person available in case that person is away?

- Do staff feel motivated to support trans people in the workplace?

- Do staff feel safe to blow the whistle if they think someone in management is behaving inappropriately in relation to company policy on trans people?

- Do staff feel confident enough to talk openly about trans issues, including any concerns they may have around the possible impact of equality policy on commercial interests?

- Are you engaging with trans people in developing and monitoring your equality policies?

- Are you keeping track of how trans people are experiencing the workplace and any concerns they have raised?

- Is there a system in place to make sure that any really serious concerns are quickly escalated to the top level?

Chapter 4

Recruitment and Dismissal

An inclusive recruitment process

Many trans people have bad experiences when applying for jobs. If they disclose that they are trans on applications, they may find that they have to send out a lot more applications than the average person before they are invited to interview. If they don't disclose, they may face hostility or ridicule when they get to interview. If they don't disclose and the interviewer doesn't notice they are trans, they may need to out themselves in order to enable the process of background checking, potentially exposing them to hostility and ridicule after they have already made the effort to get through the interview process, along with the potential disappointment of rejection for a job they thought they were about to get.

Applicants who put themselves out there and keep on trying despite all this have already shown a lot of fortitude, which means they're likely be just the sort of people you want in your business. It's up to you to make sure that you don't inadvertently scare them off or make the process impossible for them. There are several ways that you can help to make the process less intimidating.

Advertising

If you really want to have an inclusive recruitment policy and advantage your business by making sure you have access to the widest available talent pool, you need to start by thinking about your advertising strategy. Where are you making it known that you have openings available? The mainstream press and trade journals will help you reach a lot of people, but if you want to make people from minority groups feel confident about applying, you should consider placing ads in niche publications and on websites targeting hard-to-reach groups. To reach trans people, you should be advertising jobs in the LGBT press and letting local trans and LGBT support groups know when you're looking for new applicants.

One of the easiest ways to go about this is to create a dedicated mailing list. This way you will only have to ask local organisations and small press outlets once if they would like to be informed when job opportunities become available. Even if it turns out that they don't reach anybody with the skills or qualifications necessary to apply, such organisations and press outlets will usually be pleased that you are thinking of them and this can boost your general reputation.

It's also useful to think about the design of your adverts. If you use imagery featuring people, is there a visibly trans person included in it? If there is, this can send a positive message to the LGBT community as a whole. The same applies to imagery on your website, especially on pages that deal with recruitment or promote the company more generally to prospective employees.

If you are using images of trans people, stay away from clichés like trans women putting on lipstick in front of mirrors. The simplest option is simply to use an image of a trans woman who retains some masculine facial features (trans men and non-binary people tend to be less distinctive), where she's photographed in the same way as anyone else whose image you are using. Most sizeable stock photo agencies have images of trans women wearing work clothes, and the best option of all is to use an image where a trans woman is included as part of a mixed group of people who all look enthusiastic and ready for work.

Application forms

Increasingly, employers choose to state on their application forms that they are LGBT-friendly. This is good and can definitely help, but some applicants may be concerned that it's just a tick-box exercise and doesn't necessarily mean anything when it comes to attitude, training or policy.

A more effective way to get the message across can be to make a proactive statement that spells out your openness to groups facing discrimination, such as 'Applications from lesbian, gay, bisexual and transgender people, intersex people people with disabilities and members of ethnic minority groups are encouraged.'

Research by Totaljobs, published in 2016,[24] found that 43 per cent of trans job candidates actively seek out companies that seem trans-friendly before they apply for jobs.

For non-binary people, discomfort with filling in an application form can begin when no appropriate choice of title is available. Offering the option *Mx* or *Per* (alongside *Mr*, *Ms*, *Mrs* and *Miss*) makes a clear statement about inclusivity, which is likely to make all trans applicants feel more confident. It has been suggested that it is also seen positively by female applicants, who feel they are less likely to be discriminated against on the basis of their sex when they see this. Alternatively, or additionally, you can offer an 'other' option with a blank field, which also allows people to write in titles like *Dr.*, *Prof.* or *Rev.* as appropriate.

Sometimes it's very difficult for trans people to avoid outing themselves on application forms because filling in their educational history may involve stating that they have attended a gender-segregated educational establishment. For example, a person who attended Wolverhampton Girls' High School but has a male name is almost certain to be trans. There's a limited amount you can do about issues like this, which is one reason why indicating that you are a trans-friendly employer is so important.

If the nature of your business means that you will need to make background checks that could require someone who has a Gender Recognition Certificate to disclose that they are trans, you must state this explicitly on the application form. You must also explain the reasons why you need this information. You do not need to ask for the information itself to be provided on the form, which would create a risk of exposure to third parties, but you must make it clear that it will be required before any application can be successful.

If you do not need to make background checks, you should not ask for previous names on the application form, as this can force people to come out as trans.

Interview

If you ask trans people what they feel most concerned about when applying for a job, most will tell you that it's the interview. This isn't just a result of the same nerves most people experience. It reflects an awareness that this is the stage at which they are most likely to be rejected, regardless of their qualifications or suitability for the role. Many trans people have experienced or perceived hostility from interviewers in relation to their gender presentation, and this can have a damaging effect on their confidence in subsequent similar situations. Allowances should be made for this when attempting to assess an interviewee's character and working out whether or not they will fit into the workplace.

Sometimes you may interview a trans person without knowing you have done so. Some people go through binary transitions and don't retain any visible characteristics of their old gender role afterwards. Some people simply choose not to disclose at work, and not everybody goes through a name change. There is no obligation for a person to come out as trans if they don't want to and you should never make assumptions or ask directly, as this could make them very uncomfortable. If you suspect that somebody may be trans and you want them to know that it's safe for them to talk about it with you, the best way to do this is to run through your non-discrimination policy at the end of the interview and stress that you're a forward-looking employer and you want everybody to feel welcome. You can do this in a way that puts the emphasis on your pride in your friendly workplace rather than any requirement you might have of the interviewee.

Asking directly if somebody is trans can have negative repercussions for the employer as well as the employee. If the employee believes they are being asked this because the employer wishes to discriminate, they could take legal action, and the obligation would then be on the employer to prove that no discrimination was involved.

If a person whom you believe to be trans does not decide to come out, you shouldn't take it personally. Many trans people are cautious because they have had bad experiences in the past. The Totaljobs survey referenced above found that 29 per cent of trans people felt they had experienced at least one incidence of discrimination at interview because they were trans.

Background checks and references

In most (but not all) cases, people who have transitioned will have changed their names. When an employer asks for details of any previous names at the application stage of the recruitment process, this can force trans people to come out, which may discourage them from applying and mean that you miss out on potential talent. A blind application stage is better for trans people and better for employers, as it also reduces the risk of potential discrimination claims. For this reason it is a good idea to break the process of making background checks into two stages:

- At the application stage, ask the applicant to make a declaration concerning information of legitimate importance to whether or not they are eligible for the job (e.g. whether or not they have ever been in prison or have ever been convicted of an offence involving fraud).

- At the end of the recruitment process, when you have found a candidate you are happy with, ask about previous names and go through the formal background checks.

Saving questions about names until the end of the process means trans applicants don't have to go through this process as often, and you will have had time to build up some trust during the interview. This approach can also help other vulnerable applicants, such as women who have changed their names in order to escape abusive partners and need to be confident that their information will be handled discreetly.

You can take the same approach with references, initially asking for a declaration that these are available but not asking to see the references themselves until the end of the process.

Disclosure and Barring Service (DBS) checks can be made through a confidential service that offers trans people the option of keeping their gender histories private. When requesting DBS information you should always allow time for applicants to use this process, and not expect them to submit their information to you on the same day. The number to call to access the confidential service is 0151 676 1452, and those wishing to use it also have the option of doing so by emailing sensitive@dbs.gsi.gov.uk. You should include this information on your forms.

Outsourcing recruitment

If you outsource recruitment to a professional recruitment company, you still have a responsibility to make sure that the process is fair to trans applicants. Ask the companies you are considering to provide you with information on how they approach these issues and what kind of training they give to their staff. Ask for references and see what other companies have to say about them. You can also ask if they have any testimonials or recommendations from trans or LGBT organisations.

Sometimes using recruitment agencies is a problem because the agency is financially motivated to present you with candidates you are happy to accept. This means that the agency may hesitate to suggest trans candidates because it expects you to be uncomfortable about employing them. For this reason, it's very important to make it clear to recruitment agencies that you genuinely value diversity and are not just saying so because it's good public relations (PR). If the agency doesn't understand this, you could potentially miss out on a lot of talent.

What the law says

Under the provisions of the Equality Act (2010),[26] it is illegal to discriminate against an applicant at any stage in the recruitment process on grounds relating to transgender status. This is treated as a health matter, so in the event of charges being brought, the emphasis is on the employer to prove that no discrimination occurred. Having a clear written policy that shows support for trans people during the recruitment process can potentially prove useful in this situation.

Even before the Equality Act (2010) came into force, trans people had some protection in employment discrimination cases because of the relation of gender reassignment to health. In a case in 1998, an applicant who was not called for an interview by an airline successfully demonstrated that this was due to her gender reassignment and received £70,000 in compensation.[27] This stemmed from a European Court of Justice ruling made in 1996, which stipulated that the prohibition on discrimination on the grounds of sex should cover not just the state of being male or female but also the process of gender reassignment.[28]

It is unlawful to ask any job applicant questions about their health before making a firm offer of employment, and this extends to asking a trans person whether or not they have had, or are planning to undergo, surgery. You will not be in trouble if somebody volunteers this information, as some trans people do because they want to be upfront about their circumstances, but you should in no way pressure them to do so.

If a trans person volunteers the fact that they intend to go through a medical transition in the near future, at either the application or interview stage, you should thank them for being open with you and note the support that you are able to offer, but return your focus to discussing the job as soon as you are able to do so. This sends a clear message that you are not hostile to trans people or transition, and that what is important to you is the professional relationship you share with your prospective employee.

Is your recruitment strategy up to scratch?

To determine whether or not you're getting it right when it comes to recruitment, ask yourself these questions:

- Have you made it clear that trans people are welcome to apply?

- Have you made sure that people can fill in the initial application form without having to come out as trans?

- Have you allowed time for DBS checks to be made without forcing people to come out?

- Have you spoken to other people involved in the recruitment process to make sure that they will be sensitive to the needs of trans applicants?

Equality monitoring

The government strongly recommends that all businesses have an equality-monitoring strategy in place at the recruitment stage. This should begin with asking employees to fill out a form that is processed separately from the application form. For advice on handling material like this, see Chapter 5.

When it comes to trans people, it's important to think carefully about the questions you ask so that you can get useful data without putting off potential applicants. It is now becoming standard practice to ask applicants if they have a gender different from the sex they were assigned at birth. This very open question means you can identify the full range of trans employees with minimal intrusiveness. You should not ask questions with a medical focus and it is good practice to provide a 'decline to answer' option, which can also be useful to non-trans people who feel uncomfortable with the question for religious or personal reasons.

When you ask for data on sex, it is best practice to offer *male* and *female* options alongside a *non-binary* option and an *other* option accompanied by a blank field for the applicant to fill in. This illustrates that you do not think of male and female as the only two really significant genders, whilst also demonstrating your willingness to respect people's self-definition. Combining this question with the question of whether the person has a gender different from the sex they were assigned at birth means that the applicants can, if they wish, clearly indicate that they are trans men, trans women or non-binary people.

New trans employees

If a new employee has come out to you during the recruitment process, you should not assume that this means they will be happy with everybody in the company knowing about their trans status. You could, in fact, be breaking the law if you disclose that status without their permission. At the earliest opportunity you should talk to them to ask if they want to be openly trans at work, and, if so, whether or not they would like your help in introducing themselves as trans, and, if so, how you should go about that. If they don't wish to be open with everybody, you can ask if it would be helpful for a few select people to know, such as an HR contact or a first-aider.

Sometimes coming out is a practical necessity from the trans person's point of view. Joe, a trans man, had worked with troubled young people before later getting a job with Victim Support that brought him into contact with the court system. After seeing one of his previous clients during a court visit, he realised that there was a risk of such a person accidentally outing him, because the young people had known him when he was transitioning and, though supportive, didn't have much understanding of how other people might react to it or why he might prefer to keep that part of his history private. To make sure there wouldn't be a problem if this happened, he decided it would be better to come out to his team, and went to talk to his manager about it.

Unfortunately, Joe's manager didn't see his point of view. Joe put in a formal complaint and the manager ended up leaving. Joe recounts what happened:

> She said 'Why on earth would you want to do that?' like there was something shameful. She ended up bullying me. It was very upsetting. I don't deliberately live a stealth life. The idea of being told I couldn't tell people, when for me it was a question of emotional safety and the organisation was Victim Support, the irony was spectacular.

He stresses that the organisation itself was in fact supportive and backed him up.

Where an employee *does* prefer to keep their gender history private, your role as an employer is simply to ensure that their personal data is protected. See Chapter 5 for advice on how to make sure your systems are up to the task.

Dismissing an employee

Unpleasant as it is, employers sometimes have to deal with dismissing employees whose performance isn't up to scratch. When you dismiss a trans employee, there is always a possibility of discrimination being alleged, and even if this doesn't come to court, it can be very damaging. It can also cause a lot of distress to a trans person if they think they have been dismissed due to prejudice when in fact the official reasons given are genuine, and it can be all too easy for people who have experienced a lot of prejudice to come to the wrong conclusion. What can you do to reduce these risks?

The best way to manage a situation like this is to have clear policies on capability and conduct that can be easily accessed by any employee who wants to read them. These must by applied consistently and fairly, and clear records of dismissals should be kept so that this can be monitored and reviewed as required. Fairness must take into account any reasonable adjustments that might be made to remedy the situation, as an alternative to dismissal, if a trans employee's capacity has been affected by health issues – for example, if a trans woman in a manual occupation has declined in strength to the point where she can no longer safely do her job, but she could still work safely in a related role available within the company.

Where possible, dismissed employees should be encouraged to leave feedback on how the disciplinary process was handled so that this can contribute to monitoring and policy reviews. This can help you to identify mistakes if you have accidentally given the impression that you dismissed an employee because they are trans.

Providing references

If you are asked to provide a reference for a former employee who was openly trans whilst working for you, you should never assume that they are open with their prospective new employer. You should make no mention of them being trans, simply writing about a trans man or trans woman the same way you would write about any other man or woman. In the case of a non-binary person who was not referred to as *he* or *she* when working for you, it is best to contact them directly, if possible, to ask what pronouns they would prefer you to use in this context.

If you are asked for a reference for somebody who has transitioned after leaving your business, you should again aim to make contact with them directly so you can determine how they would be most comfortable with you presenting their information. If you can't do so, you should use language that aligns with the name and title they are now using, so that you don't give away the fact that they have transitioned.

Chapter 5

Data Management
Jane Fae

Data issues

Businesses can sometimes become too concerned with the fine print of their legal obligations. However, that's not to say you should ignore the law, since the law and best practice, particularly when it comes to staff and customers, tend to be on the same side.

The bottom line, legally, is that customers should all be treated equally, and businesses should not be putting in place obstacles, by accident or design, that make it harder for them to do business with you. The same applies to staff: what the law requires, and what best practice is recognised to be, is removing barriers that get in the way of working for you, so allowing you to get the best from those available.

That may sound intuitively obvious, but the greatest barrier to achieving it is 'fossilised thinking'. 'We've always done it this way; why should we change?' and 'There is no alternative' are both instances of such a mind-set. IT departments, as well as staff responsible for designing both internal and customer-facing systems, need to be challenged to explain how the solution they have come up with meets the needs of all customers, including trans ones – and if they cannot, to prove that no alternative is practically possible.

To clarify, the basic legal principles when it comes to staff and customers are:

- Don't treat any individuals less favourably because they are transgender (Equality Act 2010).[29]

- If someone complains about the way they have been treated, don't penalise them for complaining (Equality Act 2010).

- Protect their privacy: both specifically, in respect of their gender (Gender Recognition Act 2004),[30] and in respect of their personal privacy (United Nations *Universal Declaration of Human Rights*, Article 12).[31]

The impact of the Data Protection Act

In addition to legal requirements already covered, businesses should be aware of the Data Protection Act 1998 (DPA 1998)[33] and of their obligations under this legislation. Employers should note that the DPA 1998 does not set out in precise detail what is required. Rather, it lays down eight basic principles, to which businesses should conform when dealing with the personal data of employees and customers. These require that personal data be:

- fairly and lawfully processed

- processed for specified reasons

- adequate, relevant and not excessive

- accurate and, where necessary, kept up to date

- not kept for longer than is necessary

- processed in line with the rights of the individual

- kept secure

- maintained only in countries that uphold the same data processing principles.

The DPA 1998 also makes clear that processing should not cause damage or distress to individuals. This means businesses need to be aware of, and sensitive to, the range of issues that may arise in respect of trans people – particularly when it comes to recording data relevant to personal identity (name and gender).

In addition to the DPA 1998, businesses should now be preparing for the EU General Data Protection Regulation (GDPR).[32] Although the United Kingdom has decided to leave the EU, the UK government has indicated that it still intends to comply with the GDPR, which is due to come into effect in May 2018.

Businesses should be aware of, and prepare for, the fact that the GDPR will strengthen existing Data Protection obligations in a number of ways, including:

- greater penalties for breaches

- a requirement for businesses to account for how data is processed and to show that it is being processed within the law.

The GDPR also accords a broader range of rights to the individual, including:

- the right to be informed
- the right of access
- the right to rectification
- the right to erasure
- the right to restrict processing
- the right to object.

The general thrust of these obligations is that individuals have significant rights over how their data is used and maintained, and explicit consent is required for any non-obvious use to which data may be put. These, together with new rights in respect of automated decision-making and profiling, may prove disruptive for businesses that have grown used to treating individual data as theirs with which to do more or less as they please.

This is particularly important in the trans context, given that many trans people do object to the way in which their data is processed. Once these rights come into effect it is likely that some individuals will object and force change on organisations. Objections will fail where an organisation is able to show necessity for collecting specific data or processing it in the way proposed.

As explained later in this section, however, *necessity* has a very specific meaning in law: it is not sufficient for a business simply to state that it needs to do certain things. For this reason businesses need to future-proof systems, to ensure that they do not just comply with current legal requirements but that they can also adjust easily and quickly to comply with likely new obligations.

A good source of answers to specific questions in respect of the DPA is the Information Commissioner's Office (see the Further Information section at the end of this book), which runs a live chat advice service for businesses and hosts seminars on key topics, as well as maintaining a wide range of fact sheets on its online site.

Key issues for trans people regarding data management

Trans people are often very sensitive about revealing personal information – and not without reason. For a trans person, gender history is frequently a matter of embarrassment or distress: a reminder of a past they have put behind them.

'Outing' a trans person – that is, disclosing their trans history and/or identity to other members of staff or to the public without warning or consent – may not only cause embarrassment but in some circumstances also put individuals at risk of physical harm.

In many instances, problems arise as a result of insensitive handling of data around individual gender. For example:

- making disclosure of gender a requirement for doing business with your organisation

- refusing to accept a customer, or subjecting them to intrusive inquiry, because of some inconsistency in their gender details

- allowing employees access to their colleagues' gender history with no legal or business justification for such disclosure

- persistent or avoidable misgendering, which can include:

  ◦ ignoring, denying or failing to accept what an individual tells you about their gender

  ◦ creating systems that cannot handle non-standard gender data and titles – or can only do so with great difficulty

- making it (disproportionately) difficult for individuals to change gender-related markers within your system, through:

  ◦ unclear or inflexible processes

  ◦ an insistence that trans people provide more information or 'proof' than non-trans people

  ◦ a requirement for superfluous additional proofs of gender and/or identity

  ◦ making it even more difficult for (trans) people who object to your data collection process.

Issues frequently arise where people are expected to fit in with existing systems and processes and not the other way round. A system that embodies a traditional view of gender, and assigns all individuals to either *male* or *female* categories, will find it impossible to deal with someone who is non-binary.

Kit is a trans man who worked in a museum and initially came out as non-binary. He says:

I had a meeting with HR and tried to get them to update my name in records. Our leave system is designed so that it's pink or blue depending on gender. I said, 'Can this please be changed to offer a non-binary option and can you change it to male in the meantime?' They said it went to HMRC [Her Majesty's Revenue and Customs] so there was a massive misconception about tax records that dragged on for months and months. I was distressed because it was a very female-coded log screen that I had to do in front of colleagues. I eventually got them to change it when I threatened them with going to the media.

The computer says no is not merely a practical problem. Employers and service providers whose systems – from simple application form to computer database – create specific disadvantages for trans people are breaking the law. Necessity is a valid justification. It needs to be treated with caution, however, for even where the ultimate objective (e.g. security) is justified, if the individual using these systems can show that there are alternative non-discriminatory means of achieving the same result, it is likely that the systems are still unlawful.

Special measures

A further issue may arise as the result of good intentions: special measures put in place to preserve the confidentiality of trans people can have the unintended consequence of identifying an individual as trans and/or creating additional barriers to interacting with an organisation.

Both the Department of Work and Pensions (DWP) and HMRC have put in place systems to preserve the anonymity of trans individuals. Typically, these work by hiding data on the individual whose record is being queried from anyone not specifically authorised to see it. This can make ordinary interaction in Job Centres or over the phone difficult, if not impossible. In one instance, it was reported that because Job Centre staff were barred from accessing data on a particular trans individual they concluded, wrongly, that the case was fraudulent, and called the police.

Individual differences

It is important also to understand that no two trans people are exactly the same in the way they deal with the challenges and experiences of being trans. Some will be wholly 'out' and most likely proud of their gender history; others will have lived a long time 'in stealth', and deliberately or inadvertently 'outing' them may be both traumatic and dangerous for them.

Where people are in their personal 'transition journey' is relevant, as this will vary greatly by individual, and will create different challenges for a business at different stages. In general, early transition is about change: individuals are changing within themselves, and are also needing to change their official personas. Bank records, phone records, employment records – all of these will need to be changed, and although it is hoped that the amount of effort involved in each change will be minimal, the cumulative effort of making these changes can be exhausting – especially where even a small number of organisations put up unnecessary roadblocks.

The challenge to organisations is to make that transition as smooth and effortless as possible.

For those who have been transitioned for a long time, the primary objective is simply getting on with life: that may or may not involve sharing their trans backgrounds with work colleagues and friends. The important point here is that what they share and when and how they choose to do so is their decision. For organisations, the challenge is to preserve confidentiality, and to ensure that they do not suddenly find their lives disrupted because internal systems have 'leaked' personal information to their co-workers.

Stella, a trans woman who works in environmental transport, says:

> In 2013 I came out to my boss. He was really supportive and said he'd put me into the correct process, but the process was completely useless. I was asked for my GRC. I knew that was wrong, but they didn't know that I couldn't have one of those for some time. I didn't really know what correct process was. I was about to get an award for 25 years of service within the company and they wanted to put my old name on it.

What should be clear from this is that trying to treat *all* trans individuals as though they fit some stereotypical view of transition – or over-focusing on the transition process itself – can be inappropriate. When in doubt, the best policy is to ask: just ask the individual how they wish to be treated and, as far as you are able, adapt to that.

Best practice

To get back to the point made at the beginning of this chapter, not breaking the law is a good general rule of thumb.

Getting enmeshed in an argument about whether your business has or has not breached this or that legislation in respect of individual rights is time-consuming, bad for your reputation and ultimately, if it is found that you did, expensive.

The golden standard for business, however, should not be a narrow adherence to the law, with grudging acceptance that certain concessions must be made and therefore making them with bad grace and half-heartedly. Rather, best practice lies in recognising that respecting the rights of individuals and seeking to make everyone welcome is ultimately good for your business.

Along the way, you may find yourself asking some fundamental questions about how you do business: are your current systems really necessary? Or are they the way they are because that is how they have always been – unchanged because no-one has thought to question them or, often, because no-one has found the time to update them?

Along the way, you may find that what serves trans employees and customers well also works well for non-trans people.

Is gender data necessary?

We are all so used to focusing on gender that we often forget that society has moved on. The number of places where it is legally permissible – let alone socially acceptable – to offer different products and services on the basis of gender (effectively, to discriminate in terms of gender) has dwindled and shrunk. We no longer consider it acceptable for pubs to have men-only lounges. Nor is discrimination permitted across a range of financial services: it is not simply that a woman can now obtain a bank loan without her husband's permission; different rates may no longer be offered for mortgages, insurance or pensions.

This raises a basic question for every business still collecting gender data – still holding onto forms with tick-boxes labelled 'M' and 'F'- and that is, *why* are you collecting it?

Of course, it is still permitted to treat individuals differently according to gender, where it is deemed that being a particular sex is essential for a job 'for reasons of privacy and decency or where personal services are provided'.[34] However, such cases are very much the exception.

It would make far more sense to turn this issue on its head, and assume that there is no need to collect gender data *unless* there is a good identified reason to do so. This has a number of consequences, for everyone, and not just trans people.

It takes gender out of the equation when it comes to recruitment. Increasingly, the advice given to job-seekers is to omit gender from their curriculum vitae (CV). There are plenty of good reasons why an individual should do this, not least because research suggests that (unconscious) bias on the part of some businesses can harm not just the interviewee (because individuals of one or other gender are less likely to be interviewed), but also the business, as the recruitment pool has been limited.

It also removes the temptation from marketers to market products on the basis of gender, which again is often self-defeating. For instance, a recent non-gendered children's game based around fantasy-themed imagery was introduced to the United Kingdom from France. The original advertising copy talked of how this game appealed to all children of a certain age, yet the UK agency amended this to 'boys only', thereby explicitly reducing the potential market by 50 per cent.

This thinking is also problematic with more gendered products. Lingerie, for example, is bought by men as well as women, for a number of reasons, including as a gift. The strongest predictor of future purchase in this case is not necessarily gender, but whether or not an individual has previously bought a particular product.

What about title?

Many individuals view their title (e.g. *Mr, Ms, Dr*, etc.) as integral to their name and to who they are. The correct use of title is therefore a simple token of respect for an individual.

Getting it wrong is likely to create two issues. Misgendering an individual by applying the wrong title is a form of discrimination, and insisting on doing so after you have been asked to stop is both harassment and a breach of the DPA 1998. It is also likely to lead to a breakdown in relations with the individual concerned.

Over the years we have encountered business managers who have expressed surprise at, or even objected to, the vehemence with which trans individuals react to repeatedly being written to using the wrong title. What managers need to understand is that such an action is widely viewed as insulting, and persisting in using the wrong title after being asked not to is therefore rude and deliberately provocative. Blaming 'the system' is not good enough.

Issues are likely to arise where systems are based on data tables that force individuals to select a title from a pre-set list. This results in poor customer experience, and is also inefficient in IT terms. Use of free data entry for title is always preferable, as this not only allows you to accommodate the wide variety of military, academic, professional and courtesy titles that individuals may select, but also future-proofs your systems against the introduction of new titles.

For instance, one title used initially by non-binary individuals but now increasingly by trans and non-trans individuals is *Mx*. This allows an individual to present their name without simultaneously disclosing their gender, which may be an issue for non-trans women living on their own, or, in the case of non-binary individuals, incorrectly labelling themselves with a binary-gendered title. Many large organisations have now amended their systems to allow the use of *Mx* and, in some cases, other non-standard titles as well.

A further source of friction arises from marketing systems that 'predict' most likely individual gender based on first name, age and household composition. These same systems also often assign a title based on known or predicted gender.

However, as individual gender expression becomes more fluid, the use of such systems could be discriminatory. Organisations should therefore be very careful when attempting to predict data and should actively review existing systems to ensure that they are not inadvertently building gender discrimination into their businesses.

Businesses should now think carefully about how and whether they collect gender data. In many instances it may turn out to be significantly less necessary than they think.

This will benefit all customers, as well as have the effect of reducing barriers to trans people interacting with and being part of your business.

Information on 'past gender'

Collecting data on an individual's 'past gender' is in effect a demand that an individual disclose whether or not they are trans, and is likely to place an organisation in breach of both the Equality Act and the DPA. Our experience is that most organisations would never ask such a question explicitly, and would be surprised to discover that they had done so in this way.

However, past data may creep into systems in two ways. First, if a trans individual has persistent issues dealing with a call centre, they may agree, under pressure, to staff at the call centre recording in the comments section of their record that they are trans. This is effectively proof that the individual is unable to receive equal treatment from an organisation without outing themselves and is prima facie evidence of discrimination. It also creates issues of security and privacy.

In addition, an unintended consequence of storing and/or archiving gender-related information is that this may disclose changes to gender status. This would breach individual privacy and could also amount to a breach of the law, either through revealing the possession of a Gender Recognition Certificate, in breach of the Gender Recognition Act 2004, or by breaching privacy obligations under Human Rights and Data Protection legislation.

We have also encountered instances where individuals have taken it upon themselves to rectify what they perceive to be a data inconsistency, amending current data to align with what was originally held, either with or without the consent of the data subject. Such an approach is fraught with difficulty. It further highlights issues that arise when a business places too much importance on recording data, since inconsistent gender data might be an error or might indicate that the individual concerned is trans.

By insisting on 'getting it right', businesses risk creating a constant trickle of dissatisfied employees and customers, trans and non-trans alike. Removing gender will remove an element of this risk.

Protecting privacy

It is not acceptable for staff to discuss the personal lives of customers or other staff. This applies equally to sharing information about an individual's gender history that they may have obtained from the organisation's systems or through interacting with them.

Similarly, employees should not disclose the gender history (or transition) of colleagues unless they have expressly indicated that they are happy for such disclosure to take place.

Jen, a trans woman living in the South of England, says:

I tried to change my name and gender on my utility bill by calling my supplier's call centre. The person I spoke to was quite rude and made some very negative comments about trans people. I complained to their manager. I was shocked and upset when that member of staff decided to start a personal vendetta against me online, making it very clear that they knew where I lived as a result of accessing my personal data online. The matter was eventually referred to the police.

Under the DPA, organisations must have identified risks to personal data that they hold and should put in place security measures to prevent any such data being compromised, either accidentally or deliberately.

Security

It is sometimes argued that gender is necessary or useful for security purposes. The argument is that when it comes to checking identity, the more points on which it is possible to challenge an individual on the personal data they provide, the greater the likelihood of exposing identity fraud.

This then becomes manifest in a number of circumstances:

- when collecting data, 'because gender might be useful for security purposes'

- on the phone, challenging trans people, particularly trans women, because their voice is considered not to match their gender marker.

This is, however, problematic for a number of reasons. The general conclusion reached by a high-level internal government review in early 2010 of how best to check individual identity, and whether to include gender as part of a personal identification algorithm, was that gender is not especially helpful in this respect. In general, almost all individuals will be uniquely identified by a combination of surname, first name/initial, address and date of birth: the proportion of the population where gender would be an effective tie-break is minuscule.

Gender is therefore *not* especially useful for detecting identity mismatch.

It is also argued that voice may be a suspicious indicator on the phone and properly trigger action up to and including suspension of a service. Gender is estimated either through individual discretion, or through the use of voice identification software. A direct result of this mind-set is that many trans people report significant difficulties in maintaining a range of financial facilities, including access to credit and banking.

A simple query over the phone leads to their account being blocked or suspended for days or even weeks. After an investigation, the block is lifted, only to be re-applied the next time they interact with the organisation concerned. This is clearly discriminatory, in the sense that trans women regularly receive a worse service than other customers and a matter on which, lawyers have advised, they would likely win if they were to sue the offending organisation.

The defence that this is 'for security purposes' would need to demonstrate not only that this approach contributed to overall security, but also that there was no better alternative approach – in terms of the Equality Act, that no more proportionate methods exist. Such a defence also implicitly acknowledges that an organisation's existing security procedures are insufficient without subjective intervention from call centre staff. This may not be the best message to send.

Rejection of any individual on the basis of voice identification is insensitive. Its impact is not limited to trans service-users, as the spread of this practice has also resulted in instances of non-trans women whose voices are deeper than the average suffering the same indignity.

It is also potentially unlawful discrimination, as it not only forces trans people to disclose their trans identity, but in many instances leads to the provision of a markedly less full service for trans individuals than for non-trans ones.

Equality monitoring

By law, many organisations are required to carry out equality monitoring. The aim of such monitoring is to enable an organisation to generate an aggregate count of specific groups, without disclosing information on specific individuals more widely within the business. This may be to ensure that they are complying with their obligations under the Equality Act or simply to gain greater understanding of the composition of the workforce. Clearly it would be appropriate, in the course of a legitimate monitoring exercise, to collect data on gender history and/or trans status. Best practice in this respect is to create an equality monitoring facility not linked to other personal data held on an individual. At interview, for example, an equality monitoring form may be distributed on an anonymised and detachable form. This can then be separated from the CV and analysed discreetly, enabling an organisation to meet its legal obligations without re-introducing gender to its recruitment procedures. This also enables businesses to monitor a range of key factors, including gender, ethnicity, and disability without making it specific to the individual.

Care should be taken to keep such information confidential – even where data has been collected anonymously and in line with best practice, there is a danger that reporting back on this data, even in aggregate form, could breach confidence. For example, if an organisation employed one black, Asian or minority ethnic employee, who was also trans and lesbian, a questionnaire that asked about race, sexuality and gender history on the same form would enable identification of the trans person straightaway.

Similarly, a report that revealed a trans person working in a small or medium-sized department would be likely to generate speculation and gossip about who that might be. In addition, taking any discriminatory action on the basis of information disclosed in such an exercise would be unlawful.

Businesses should note that for monitoring purposes 'transgender' is not a gender. Individuals may identify as trans but many will identify as male *and* trans, female *and* trans or even non-binary *and* trans.

Forms that conflate the two will therefore run into two difficulties: they will irritate those people who do not regard their gender as trans; and they will return inaccurate data, as you are forcing individuals to choose between trans and what they consider to be their actual gender.

Changing name

If your organisation or your staff talk about a 'legal name change', then it is likely that your policies in this area are not just wrong but open to challenge. Part of the problem is that the phrase has become so ingrained in corporate thinking that it is used without any understanding. As a result, policies and systems are developed on the basis of a fiction; and those same policies and systems fail to address what should be real corporate objectives in this area.

To begin with, let's consider what name change is not. It is not a 'legal change' in the sense that individuals have a legal name and some form of permission or authorisation is required to change it, as is the case in the United States or France.

In England, Scotland, Wales and Northern Ireland, there is no such thing as a 'legal name'. Unless there is some dishonest or fraudulent intent – impersonating a wealthy individual, for example, in order to access their bank account – your name is simply what you call yourself. It is established through usage – if you call yourself 'John Smith' and are known to your friends and colleagues as John Smith, then that is your name. You may even choose more than one name.

The same applies to your title – though here some additional caveats are in operation. How you are addressed – as *Mr*, *Mrs*, *Miss* or *Mx* – is entirely up to you, and refusal to recognise an individual's choice of title, or putting up unreasonable barriers before you will allow them to use a particular title, is likely to be discriminatory.

Unlike the use of name, some restrictions on the use of title exist. Certain professional titles, such as *engineer* or *orthoptist*, are protected. They are marked in UK names through the addition of post-nominal letters, and it is an offence punishable by a fine of up to £5,000 to lay claim to a professional title to which one is not entitled.

The question of whether titles such as *Sir* or *Lady* are 'protected' is somewhat murkier. Anyone who takes on a title that implies either noble or social rank with the intention of misleading others is likely committing a fraud, but if John Smith merely wishes to be called Sir John

Smith, such a practice is permitted – and recognised by the UK passport office, which will happily issue a passport in which *Sir* is included as a first name (and not as a title).

While this is a somewhat arcane topic, it reinforces the suspicion that when organisations talk about 'legal name change' they are not focused on the real legal requirements involved. Extensive barriers are put up in respect of individuals who wish to change their title from *Mr* to *Miss*, or even *Miss* to *Mrs*, which is nowhere subject to legal sanction, while little or no attention is paid to whether an individual is permitted to use a particular protected title, which *is* regulated by law.

Organisations also need to understand that name change does not engage any particular legal process. This follows naturally from the fact that individual names are whatever people choose to call themselves. An individual who has decided to change their name from John Smith to Jane Smith and is known by the latter name to their colleagues is 'legally' Jane Smith, with or without any supporting documentation such as deed poll or statutory declaration. Individuals do not therefore need 'a legal document' in order to change their name.

The real issue for most organisations is security/identity. For example, an individual known to you by one name and accessing a range of privileges under that name has requested that you grant access to the same set of items under their new name. Where they are a new employee, there is no issue: they will present themselves to your organisation using whatever name they have decided to use, and so long as they have supporting documentation (e.g. driving licence and passport) providing evidence of that identity, you should accept that documentation. This is straightforward. However, we are aware of instances where organisations have required trans people to provide additional supporting documentation over and above what they would request from non-trans people. This is unlawful.

The proofs of identity required in respect of a name change should be proportionate to the impact of that change. For name change on membership of a dance club, a simple signed letter may suffice: for name change on significant financial assets, biometric or secure password details may be more appropriate.

Where a member of staff changes name, provided it is clear that they are doing so consistently across all records, it is likely to be very inappropriate to challenge this or demand 'proof' before you accept the change. For example, if John Smith now wishes to be known as Jane Smith, it should be sufficient for them to make that request to their line manager or to a member of the HR department to whom they are known personally – and for the latter simply to implement the name change.

A genuine security focus means identifying continuity: obtaining proofs that an individual is the same individual pre- and post-name change. That may involve biometrics, personal recognition (appropriate in the workplace) or simply presentation of a uniquely coded document carrying pre- and post-change name versions: for example, a tax return showing old and new names as well as the person's National Insurance number.

Excessive demands for proofs in respect of name change may constitute unlawful discrimination – especially where an organisation requires an individual to obtain a deed poll or statutory declaration for which they must spend money. For this reason, too, organisations should always retain such documentation safely and securely and return it to the individual at the end of the process.

Changing gender

There are a small number of services where gendered provision is permitted[35] and gender therefore matters. Otherwise, as argued earlier in this chapter, gender is a weak indicator for identification purposes and it is unclear, when it comes to changing gender markers, why an individual should be required to 'prove' anything to an organisation other than that they would like that organisation to change existing gender markers and related information so as to match their identified gender.

A particular issue arises in respect of change of gender where an organisation asks trans employees and service-users to provide sight of their Gender Recognition Certificate before they will agree to change name, title or gender. This is likely to be unlawful discrimination and/or harassment contrary to the Equality Act, while requesting sight of a Gender Recognition Certificate or even asking a person if they have one before agreeing to change just gender-related information may well be a specific and potentially expensive breach of the Gender Recognition Act.

Yoyo changes

Annette, a trans woman who works as a software engineer, recalls the early stages of her transition at work:

> A lot of the time was spent doing IT things, changing usernames and so on. That went smoothly but because we're a tech company there was a lot to do. Some systems handled it better than others. Some treated it as 'a new user has been created' so stuff had to be copied over. For a couple of weeks the odd thing would turn up and even a few months later a colleague said when they forwarded my email my name appeared wrong. It turned out to have been caused by an obscure setting and we had to go in and change it manually.

It is highly frustrating for customers to change some aspect of their personal information, only for the change mysteriously to undo itself some months or years later. For example, a business changes a customer address, gets the address right for two years – and then simply reverts to the old address. This is especially the case for trans people, who may have expended significant effort getting name and gender data changed within an organisation's systems, only for it to go back to what it was held as before, suddenly and without explanation. And while the consequence of address data returning to what it was some years back may cause annoyance and irritation, the consequence for a trans person of gender data suddenly reverting can be far more serious, outing them to people unaware of their past history and potentially placing them in real physical danger.

There are two common reasons why this may occur. Often, changes are applied only to current data, and not to previous data history or archived data. As a result, if the system needs to be reset to a point before the change took place, or old data are re-accessed, then the result will be as though the change was never implemented.

Organisations should therefore always be very careful, when restoring systems from archive data, that old names and titles are not carried forward.

The second reason that changes may not 'stick' within an organisation is because that organisation uses multiple systems: for marketing, for accounting, for services, etc. When updating name and gender data, the change may only be implemented on one or two systems, with the result that when the third system is accessed, no change will have been made.

Alternatively, the change is carried out on some systems – but the business later decides to update all records from an internal source that has not been updated, and which over-writes updated data with non-updated data.

Best practice for all organisations is the implementation of a single view, whereby all personal data are maintained in the form of a single aggregated, consistent and full representation.

Checklist

Whether you're dealing with customers or employees, best practice will often amount to the same thing. Here are some simple questions to ask of your organisation to determine whether or not it is applying best practice in the area of gender:

Question	Best practice
Do you *need* to record gender?	If you can't demonstrate both commercial and legal justification for doing so, don't.
Are you recording past gender?	The first and most important question is: do you need to? There is rarely justification for doing so.
	Where organisations find that their systems do so inadvertently, they should ensure that any data that cannot be amended, rewritten or reissued, which would reveal the past gender status of a person, is concealed.
Do you have policies in place regarding information on past gender?	Information on gender and gender history should be available on a 'need to know basis' only.
	HR may need to keep track of an individual's gender history. However, if that individual is not 'out' within your organisation, you should consider carefully whether their line manager needs to know.
Do you have adequate security in place to protect sharing of past gender information?	Ensure that a co-worker cannot inadvertently stumble across a file that includes protected information. For example, hard copy should be stored securely and separately from other staff records, and clearly marked to show who is authorised to deal with its contents, should the need arise.
	Access to such information should also always be with the permission of the person concerned, except in emergencies.
	Online records that might reveal past gender status must be password protected and, again, only accessible in certain circumstances, by persons authorised to access such data.
Are the processes for changing data straightforward and simple?	The more process surrounding issues such as change of name, the more likely it is that a system will maintain data on gender history and the more likely that privacy will be breached.
Does your complaint process make matters worse?	Your complaint process should never result in an individual being victimised, either directly through less favourable treatment of the individual, or indirectly through making their trans status visible.
	All too often, this can happen where the complaint process is overly bureaucratic and/or formal.

The bottom line: stay flexible

In the end, good business practice is about providing great customer experience and creating an excellent workplace. This will not be achieved by forcing people to adapt to your process and your way of doing things.

Respecting individual wishes will pay dividends, and businesses that seek to fit to the needs of others will ultimately prove more successful than those determined to make others conform to their world view.

For details of organisations providing information on transgender issues in the workplace, please see the Further Information section at the end of this book.

Chapter 6

Transgender People in the Workplace

Common problems faced by trans people at work

Research published by Totaljobs in 2016[36] found that 60 per cent of trans people in the United Kingdom have encountered some kind of transphobic discrimination at work. This may be intentional or unintentional, but either way, it risks making trans employees feel unwelcome and unable to function effectively within the workplace.

The sooner you tackle discrimination within your workplace, the easier it will be to get rid of it. If it's ignored, it can spread among employees who were not initially hostile, and can become a habit that people find difficult to break even if they want to. You should take a firm stance from the start and make it clear that you will not tolerate any kind of bullying – but, at the same time, let your other employees know that you are willing to discuss any concerns they may have. It's much easier to resolve problems when you can get at the root cause.

Helping other employees to adjust

Some employees may, sadly, react to a trans colleague coming out with hostility or mockery, but others may have genuine concerns. Although the trans person is likely to need the most support, taking the time to address others' concerns can help to ensure that everything goes as smoothly as possible.

Most concerns about working alongside a trans person stem from ignorance. For example, people may mistakenly believe that being trans is a sexual fetish, leading them to feel sexually threatened. Directing your staff to websites where they can learn more about trans people can allay these concerns (please see the Further Information section at the end of this book). It also means that they will have an opportunity to enhance their understanding without bothering their trans colleague with a lot of questions. Some trans people don't mind dealing with questions, but others, understandably, want to be able to get on with their jobs with as little fuss as possible.

Religious and political objections

You may find that some people in your workplace object to the presence of trans people on a religious or political basis. Although everybody is entitled to their privately held views, everyone should recognise that there are some things it is not appropriate to express in the workplace. If you are confronted with this sort of objection, you need to explain politely but firmly that they don't need to agree with every aspect of how their fellow employees live in order to treat them politely and respectfully, and nobody should deliberately be made to feel uncomfortable at work.

Sometimes you may be required to make decisions that balance the rights of trans employees against the rights of other employees to practise their religion. Real conflicts like this are rare, however, because most of the time there is a simple way to accommodate both sets of needs. It can be helpful to talk to religious leaders in your local community in order to get advice that the religious employee will find clear and acceptable. Often people have a more extreme idea of what their religion requires of them than is really the case, and their leaders can reassure them that, for example, they are not betraying their religious principles by working alongside trans people and addressing them using their preferred pronouns. Most major religions stress the importance of obeying national laws, so it can be helpful to stress that non-discrimination against trans people is a matter of law and not solely a matter of company policy.

It's useful to note that international human rights law incorporates a principle of plurality and tolerance, in accordance with which there is no right to protection from being offended. If a trans employee upsets a religious employee, for example by repeatedly asserting that their beliefs are morally wrong, and doing so in a manner calculated to produce distress, that could constitute harassment, in which case the trans employee would be at fault. No employee, however, is responsible for others feeling offended simply because of their existence or presence in the workplace.

When you are trying to strike a balance between different sets of rights at work, you should take account of the following human rights principles:

- Proportionality – any restrictions on the right to manifest religious beliefs or the right to express gender must have a legitimate aim and be achieved through means that are proportionate and necessary. You should always aim to restrict people as little as possible in order to arrive at a solution that doesn't significantly inconvenience anyone and is acceptable to both sides.

- Respect for others to believe – in trying to ensure that religious people have their views fairly taken into account, you don't have to share those beliefs or think that they are sensible. The beliefs themselves are not a stakeholder; the believer is. In respecting that individual employees believe what they do, you can aim to develop solutions that fit people rather than trying to make people fit rules.

- No hierarchy of rights – no protected characteristic under the Equality Act[39] is held to be more important than any other. You should work to ensure that each employee has their rights respected to the maximum degree possible. No right should be lightly set aside or considered trivial in relation to another.

Discussing these principles and the obligations they place on you as an employer can be a good starting point for getting employees to cooperate in finding a solution rather than refusing to give ground. You should always focus on how specific interactions can be better managed, rather than asking either party to try to change who they are. Be careful to take into account the differing levels of self-esteem that your employees may have. Sometimes one person will offer to make major concessions in order to keep the peace, but will find the result, if accepted, difficult to deal with as time goes on.

Political beliefs do not have the same protection as religious beliefs. This includes arguments that might seem to relate to other protected characteristics, such as the belief among some feminists that the acceptance of trans women is damaging to other women. If a female employee is concerned for her personal safety, for example in regard to sharing toilet facilities with a trans woman, and this belief persists after she has had training about trans people, you can look for a solution such as arranging for somebody else to accompany her at times when she feels unsafe (such a solution should not interfere with the trans woman going about her day-to-day activities like anyone else); but if her concerns are more general, she should refrain from expressing them in a way that negatively affects her trans colleagues.

Training

Most employers do not feel very confident about providing training on trans issues themselves, and this is entirely reasonable – if you don't know the subject back to front, it's easy to make mistakes, and mistakes could leave you with a whole new set of problems. It's much better to find someone who can deliver professional training.

Some individual trans people offer training in their local areas. This can be cheaper than dealing with an organisation, but quality varies a lot, and some individuals are really only able to talk about their own experiences.

Whilst this can still help – your employees are more likely to recognise that trans people are human like them if they have an opportunity to engage with a trans person who doesn't mind answering their questions – it can mean that some important issues don't get covered at all, or that the trainer makes sweeping statements based on personal experience that don't really apply more generally. If you're considering bringing in an individual, ask for references and see what other companies say about them.

If you bring in a large organisation such as Stonewall, Galop or the Equality Network (see the Further Information section at the end of this book), you can get professional quality training which will cover all the bases and be better able to take account of issues specific to your type of workplace. You could also look at what local charities and support groups can offer you. The advantage of going local is that, as well as keeping the cost down, it often makes it easier for your employees to relate to the trainer and discover they have things in common, which helps to make training effective and memorable.

Whatever form of training you use, make sure to gather feedback from your employees. This can help you to identify any areas where further work might be needed.

If employees are reluctant to attend training sessions like these, remind them that they can mention having attended them on their CVs to make themselves more employable in future. You can also link attendance at sessions like these to eligibility for promotion within your company. Explain that asking them to attend training doesn't mean that you think they're hostile to trans people. If you can, draw on examples from your own experience to explain how easy it is for a well-intentioned person to misunderstand something, and remind them that attending training is also in itself a good way to show support for a trans colleague.

Harassment

Employers have a duty to ensure that trans employees are not harassed by other employees. Harassment can take the form of threats but is often subtler and may, for example, involve somebody repeatedly using the wrong name or pronouns. This can happen by accident, of course, and most trans people are understanding about this; but if it persists or it becomes apparent that there is malicious intent, disciplinary procedures will have to come into force.

Researchers estimate that around 10 per cent of people react negatively to a colleague going through transition.[37] If several members of your team are vocal about not wanting to work with a trans person, and you find yourself wondering if it wouldn't be easier to find a way of getting rid of your trans employee rather than damaging your relationship with the transphobic staff, ask yourself if you really want to have a workplace where people bully each other. People who are transphobic often harbour other types of prejudice as well. Letting them get away with harassing a trans person could embolden them to harass disabled employees or employees from different ethnic backgrounds. Do you want to risk having employees who think they're in charge of recruitment and can behave however they like, or do you want a workplace where you are in charge in practice as well as in name?

Employees need to understand that they have a responsibility to help the business achieve its aims, and that harassment is a performance issue because it interferes with the efficient running of the business. Framing the problem in this way makes it clear that it's not just a personal issue, which gives you some protection in the event that a disciplined or dismissed employee takes legal action against you. It also lets you stress the damaging effect of harassment on overall productivity and morale in a small business context – it can be worth pointing out that everyone's livelihood, including that of the bully or bullies, depends on good teamwork. You can add that this isn't just about the victim being trans and that you would respond in just the same way if any other employee was harassed at work.

It's important not to lose your temper during confrontations like this. If you're frustrated by the disruption and you've been trying to work around the problem for a while, you may be feeling quite emotional, but remaining calm and authoritative will get you much better results.

Trans people and single-sex environments

In the last few years there has been a lot of discussion in the media about which toilets it's appropriate for trans people to use. There is no law in the United Kingdom restricting who uses particular toilets. In fact, the law makes it clear that trans employees have the right to use the toilets that feel most appropriate to them, and must not be made to use disabled toilets (an approach some employers have tried in the past), though they may do so by choice. Some non-binary people feel more comfortable using disabled toilets because these are usually gender neutral, and some binary trans people find this a good interim option before they have fully settled into their new role.

In workplaces where single-sex environments offer less privacy, such as changing rooms and showers that all employees need to use, employers need to take extra steps. Although trans employees still have the right to use the facilities of their choice, it's important to make sure that all employees' concerns are respected. This means that, for example, it may be necessary to install separate stalls for showers instead of having a single open area. The good news is that this is usually less expensive than assumed, and once it has been done the workplace is future-proofed and functional for any similar situations in future at no extra cost. The increased privacy is also likely to be welcomed by employees facing other bodily issues (e.g. those who wear colostomy bags).

Most people who transition at work report that their colleagues soon get used to sharing single-sex spaces with them and relax about it. Trans women say that their male colleagues seem to worry more about them using female-only spaces than their female colleagues do. Male-only spaces can feel very unsafe for trans women, even early on in transition when they don't feel confident about using female ones, especially if they have to share them with people they don't know. Because there is always a possibility of hidden issues, employers should make sure that all employees feel comfortable about approaching them with any concerns they may have.

Laura, an HR manager, felt strongly that an employee who came out to her as a trans woman should be able to use the women's toilets as she wanted to, but spent a long time talking to her in order to work out when would be the right time to make that change. She says:

I think one of the most difficult things to tackle, partly because it's so personal, is which toilets to use. I know individuals who've been pointed towards disabled toilets. That doesn't feel like supporting those individuals in the right way. If they've been brave enough to take this decision and open up, they should be supported.

Fortunately, she encountered no objections. She continues:

If I'd come up against that, I would have really struggled with it, but I think we would have got to the same end. It would have been about talking to those people and educating them.

The employee Laura was supporting went on to use the women's toilets without a problem.

Non-binary people may find toilet access particularly difficult. At present, only 25 per cent of employers offer gender-neutral toilet facilities. Employers should let their non-binary employees decide which of the available facilities represents the best option for them, and should make sure that they are supported in making a free choice. If there is a key used for accessing disabled facilities, they should be offered a copy of this. In many cases, non-binary people prefer to use women's toilets because they consider this safer.

Uniform policy

If your employees wear uniforms that differ according to sex, you will need to ensure that a new uniform is available for any employee going through a binary transition (from male to female or from female to male). This should be the same as the uniforms worn by other people living in the gender role that the employee has transitioned to, so a trans woman should wear the standard women's uniform and a trans man should wear the standard men's uniform. The only exception to this is in circumstances where safety issues apply. For example, if the uniforms designed for men do not come in a size small enough for a particular trans male employee, and this presents a risk of the uniform getting caught in machinery used in the workplace, the employer should instead aim to provide a uniform that is as close as possible to the standard men's uniform, but it does not have to be exactly the same.

New uniforms for trans employees should be provided on the same basis that a new uniform is provided when an employee goes up or down in size, so any financial contribution required from the employee must be consistent with that.

If you have a non-binary employee, best practice is to ask them which version of the uniform they would prefer. Any further changes agreed to in order to make that person's uniform less gender specific should be maintained consistently thereafter so that it's clear to other employees that it's just a different version of the uniform, not a case of special treatment that means that person gets to wear whatever they want.

In some companies, issues with the way data management systems are set up can make it very difficult for trans people to access appropriate uniforms even though nobody actually objects to them wearing them. In this situation, managers need to ensure that special provision is made, and system administrators need to be alerted to the problem and instructed to resolve it so that it doesn't cause further problems in future.

In workplaces where there is a dress code rather than a uniform, the same rough set of rules applies. Trans women should not be held to a different standard from other women and trans men should not be held to a different standard from other men. It is not acceptable to ask a trans person to dress differently just because you don't think they look good in the clothes they are wearing.

Office work

As a rule, office environments are the easiest context for trans people to come out in. Higher levels of education correlate with lower levels of prejudice, so they are more likely to find acceptance quickly. The potential for anonymity that offices create can lead to some specific kinds of problem, however, especially in larger companies. If a colleague is hostile, it's often easy for them to send bullying messages through email or the office intranet, or leave messages on the trans person's desk. Although these might seem like low-level incidents, they can cause a lot of stress if they happen repeatedly, especially if the victim doesn't know who's responsible and is therefore uncertain who they can trust.

When this kind of bullying is going on, employees should be advised to keep a log of the dates and times of any incidents, with details of anyone else who witnessed them. This can help managers to determine who is involved in any anonymous incidents. Messages sent through computers are sometimes traceable even if they appear to be anonymous. Managers should be aware that there could be more than one person involved.

A log of incidents can also help to build up a case against the perpetrator. Whilst a single comment could be dismissed as a misinterpreted joke, it's easy to show that a series of incidents mandates disciplinary action. Even if there is not enough to justify moving the bully or terminating their contract when the problem first comes to light, they can be warned that such actions will be brought to bear if their behaviour continues, and advised that they will be watched. In most situations, this is enough to resolve the problem. Most people harassing others at work do not believe that they will be caught, or do not expect their behaviour to be taken seriously.

The service sector

Trans people working in the service sector interact extensively with the public and sometimes experience transphobia from customers or clients. One common problem occurs when a customer asks to speak to the manager and says they refuse to be served by a trans person. The manager should always respond to this by backing the staff member and expressing confidence in their abilities. Often people will back down at this point. If instead they are explicit about the fact that they dislike the employee being trans, the manager should state clearly that the business does not tolerate transphobia, and ask them to leave. Employers are legally obliged to protect their employees and it is not acceptable to simply ask a different member of staff to help a customer like this. As far as the law is concerned, the customer is not always right.

Trans people should not be expected to confine themselves to backroom roles, away from the public, unless they specifically request to do so. Limiting their choice of roles more than the choice available to other workers with the same skill-set could constitute discrimination. See Chapter 8 for further advice on how to manage challenging situations involving members of the public.

Educational environments

Employees transitioning in educational environments can present additional challenges because it still attracts a measure of controversy. Employers may worry about unwanted attention from the press, but this is no reason not to support a transition, and indeed more and more people are entering the profession post-transition without complications.

In schools, children are usually very accepting, and the majority of parents present no problems. If a member of the teaching staff is transitioning, it's now common practice for schools to hold a special meeting for parents, or to send a letter round, creating an opportunity for anyone with concerns to ask questions. Naturally this should not be done unless it's something the employee is comfortable with, but it can be very effective. Parents will inevitably find out about the transition because the children will talk about it and informing them directly, in a positive way, sends a clear message that it's not something the school authorities feel should be a cause for concern.

If a school transition receives unwanted press attention, a 'no comment' approach together with a simple statement supporting the trans employee is usually the best way to defuse it. Employers should be aware that stories given to friendly reporters from local publications may be picked up by national publications and presented in a less positive way. Reporters can be reminded that the Editors' Code of Practice states that 'all pupils should be free to complete their time at school without unnecessary intrusion' (clause 6, subclause 1) and that 'they must not be approached or photographed at school without permission of the school authorities' (clause 6, subclause 2).[38]

In universities, the presence of trans people is less likely to attract concern, but there is a risk that being trans will be treated as an academic point or even a political choice, which can make things difficult for those who want to keep their personal and work lives separate. Anne has been living in a female gender role in her private life for decades but didn't feel able to come out at work until 2010, and even then waited until she had completed her probationary period at a new university in order to do so – something she believes to be commonplace. The key, she says, was the passing of the Equality Act. 'It was an absolute godsend! Suddenly I had the confidence to come out and be myself openly.'

Anne found that although it took a while for colleagues to get her name and pronouns right – something that improved noticeably once she had the full support of management – students respected her gender from the outset. She found, however, that the number of student complaints about her work increased and she felt that her appearance was policed more than that of other women in the department. Dealing with what may be unconscious prejudice has proved challenging. She has been uncomfortable about colleagues discussing academic work that calls into question the acceptance of trans people in front of her, and another incident left her questioning the sincerity of some of the support she received:

> I am told an academic was disciplined for gross professional misconduct after being transphobic towards a trans student. This individual's publication record, however, ensured that this did not result in dismissal. This suggested to me that transphobic discrimination is still not regarded as a serious issue and may be mitigated by academic stature and publication record.

Family businesses

Perhaps the most high-risk environment for a trans person to come out in is a family business. This applies whether it's run by their own family (many trans people are rejected by one or more family members when they come out) or by another family. If it goes well, it can be a wonderful experience, but if they meet with hostility, the emotional impact can be considerable. Even if most people in the business are supportive, a trans employee in this situation may not know who to talk to about hostility they face because they don't expect anybody to take their side when there are family bonds at stake.

John, a young trans man who worked in a café, says that his manager was one of the first people he came out to, and her daughter made jokes about him. He didn't get the feeling that she intended these to be hurtful, but he wishes people would think about what they say. He was also misgendered on a regular basis, with people using the wrong pronouns, and felt that he 'just had to lump it'. This kind of situation is obviously damaging to employee morale and doesn't encourage employees to stay with the company.

If you're running a family business, it's always important to make sure that you don't let personal matters get in the way of the smooth running of that business. A family member coming out as trans can obviously have a big impact, but it's your job to ensure that the business environment remains professional and that nobody, no matter what the strength of their feelings is, bullies anybody else or treats them with the kind of disrespect that makes it difficult for them to do their job.

If your family business is employing some non-family members, it's important to have a clear written policy on equality within the workplace, and another on what constitutes unacceptable behaviour. Your employees must know that they will get a fair hearing if they report problems to you, even if they are telling you that your sister or your son has done something wrong. It's difficult to discipline people you know, but it's also a skill that's essential to running a successful business of this type. Just as you may need to be tough when somebody is managing finances badly or not pulling their weight, you may sometimes need to be tough on behavioural issues, and ultimately most people will respect you as long as you are consistent and fair.

Masculine business cultures

When looking at how businesses can be more inclusive of trans people, it has to be acknowledged that some businesses still haven't got very far in being inclusive of women. Often this is despite the best efforts of managers and of those at the top of the profession. Masculine business cultures can be difficult for women to succeed in because female employees can feel very isolated and often struggle to network effectively. These environments – which exist in both blue-collar and white-collar workplaces – are also difficult places for trans people to come out in.

Annette, a software engineer, says she was worried about coming out at work partly because she didn't want to lose male privilege in an environment where there are very few women. She asked to be transferred to another team because she wanted to be in a team with another woman in it. Fortunately, she had an office manager who was female and very supportive, and this did a lot to boost her confidence.

Stella, who works in environmental transport, says that she found the masculine culture in one workplace so challenging that she felt unable to come out there for years. She says:

> It was a really macho, masculine environment and I was always putting up with misogynistic and transphobic jokes. I always felt sidelined because I didn't join in, and it put me off transitioning because I knew I'd have to out myself to all these guys. What happened then was I got sidelined into a new role in a health and safety environment. It was nine to five in an office. Most of my colleagues were female and the boss was a woman, so I decided it was safe to transition.

Changes of staff

In many companies, trans people's experiences depend on the relationships they have built up with key members of staff. Changes in staffing can present problems, and it's important for people in senior roles to be alert to this and step in where necessary.

One of the most common problems reported by trans people is difficulty arising from changes in HR personnel or immediate management. If the person who has supported the trans employee's transition or integration into the workplace leaves, all too often the support process ends too. Although the trans person may have ongoing issues and need ongoing support (e.g. to make sure that other newcomers to the workplace behave respectfully towards them), the new person entering that role may not realise this or understand its importance. This can leave trans people feeling isolated and unsure how to proceed.

The best way to prevent this problem developing is for a new immediate manager or any newcomer to a senior HR role to arrange a meeting with any trans member of staff as soon as possible. In some cases they may be told that there is nothing to worry about and no need for any extra support, but it is always best to err on the side of caution.

Employers should also be alert to the extra complications trans people can face when being moved into situations where they're working with new people, especially if they have to deal with a lot of new people at once.

Tamsin, who works in food manufacturing, was getting along well at work post-transition when she was suddenly moved onto a new shift with 50 people she didn't know. She says:

> I was placed in a vulnerable situation. The management ignored my mail about it, and I had to go through the whole process again.

___

In a situation like this, employers should recognise that it's necessary to provide the same kind of support as when the trans employee first came out at work. Tamsin had to deal with the situation alone whereas her employer should have offered to explain her situation to workers on the new shift and should have provided ongoing support to deal with any problems.

Interacting with other businesses

No matter how carefully you manage things within your own business, you can't control what other people do with theirs, and this can potentially create problems when your trans employees interact with people from other businesses. Some trans people prefer to avoid roles where this is necessary, but others complain that their managers are overly protective – they find themselves kept back from such interactions and worry that it could cost them career opportunities. Ultimately, the trans employees should be the ones making the decisions about what they can and can't cope with. They should also get to decide whether or not people in the other business are told that they are trans – you should never out them without their consent, even if your intention is to make things easier for them. If you do so, you could potentially make things a lot harder, and you could be breaking the law.

Interactions with other businesses don't always involve the obvious things like meetings or conferences. They can crop up in day-to-day situations that are often overlooked by managers. For example, a trans employee who comes into the office early may come into contact with cleaners contracted from another company, or a trans person organising stock in a warehouse may have to deal with delivery drivers. It's important to let your employee know that if they experience transphobia in these situations, they should report it just as they would when it involves a colleague.

If you receive reports of transphobic behaviour perpetrated by another company's employees, you will have to speak to the people in that other company who are responsible for supervising those employees, and make it clear that you won't tolerate such behaviour. It can help to point out that the behaviour may constitute a hate crime, so the employees could be open to prosecution, which would not do their bosses' reputation any good. Employers could be held liable for their employees' behaviour and risk being sued. In most cases you will find that the people you deal with are apologetic and either withdraw those staff from that position or undertake disciplinary measures.

See Chapter 10 for advice on how to handle relationships between businesses in different jurisdictions and businesses operating in different cultural contexts.

Employee assistance programmes

If your business contracts out an employee assistance programme (EPA), you will need to check that staff there are suitably trained to support trans people and are sensitive when doing so. Ask for references from each company you consider so you can find out what other organisations think of them. Ask what kind of training they give to their staff and make sure that they have robust equality and diversity policies. Ask if any trans or LGBT organisations can recommend them.

Always make sure that there is somebody in your organisation whom employees can turn to if they feel that the EPA is failing to address their concerns or to treat them with respect.

Training opportunities

You have a legal obligation to make sure that any training opportunities you offer are equally accessible to trans people. This means ensuring that trans employees are offered training opportunities as often as other employees (after taking into account factors like their role within the company and the amount of time they've spent there), and ensuring that the courses themselves are suitable.

If you are contracting out training, you will need to make sure that the training provider has a robust equality policy and does not discriminate or exhibit prejudice against your trans employees. It's a good idea to structure feedback forms for course attendees in a way that helps you identify any problems, not just asking how useful they found the training but asking how they felt about the way it was provided.

Promotion and transfer opportunities

To meet your obligations under the Equality Act, you will need to be able to demonstrate that you offer promotion and transfer opportunities to your trans employees on the same basis that you offer them to other employees. This includes making sure that when several employees are considered for the same promotion, the selection process is fair to any trans people under consideration. It's a good idea to think about how you are going to measure this when you design the selection process. For example, if you are going to interview candidates, devise a clear scoring system that will make it easy to monitor which qualities the interviewers think each candidate is strong or weak on. If you find that trans candidates are repeatedly given low scores for factors like presentation, speech and ability to get along with others, it's time to investigate.

In some cases, trans people may decline promotion or transfer opportunities because they believe, for example, that having a higher public profile or working with a new team could expose them to prejudice and make their lives a lot more stressful. Employers should be aware of this possibility and not assume that a reluctance to apply for such opportunities indicates a lack of ambition or loyalty to the company. If the issue comes up in discussion, you should discuss the possibility of finding opportunities that would be a better fit for the employee, or find ways of resolving concerns about existing options.

Remuneration

It might sound odd, but in a large organisation it can sometimes be difficult to keep track of what your employees are being paid. When salaries and bonuses are negotiated on an individual basis, it's easy for some employees to end up being undervalued. This can lead to trouble if it emerges that there's a pattern of discrimination, even if those involved in pay negotiations were not consciously aware that they were discriminating. It also means that valuable employees could suddenly leave you if they are headhunted or suddenly realise that they could be earning a lot more somewhere else.

Trans people are at particular risk of being undervalued, for several reasons. Perhaps most significantly, they often undervalue themselves – because the process of job hunting can be so challenging they feel grateful for having any paid work at all. If they have generally low confidence due to the effects of prejudice and discrimination – even if that's now firmly in the past – they can find it harder to assert themselves. Studies have found that men tend to be more confident than women and this is believed to be one of the reasons why men are more likely to earn higher salaries for doing the same jobs. (Sometimes, of course, confidence is a genuine business asset, but that's not always the case, and overconfident employees can easily get a business in trouble.)

Trans people also face a risk of being undervalued due to prejudice, whether conscious or unconscious, on the part of managers. This doesn't just apply to pay negotiations themselves but can mean, for instance, that they receive fewer commendations for their work, giving them less clout when the negotiations happen.

With these issues in mind, it's a good idea for employers to pay close attention to the remuneration their trans employees are receiving and make sure that it is proportionate in relation to the work they are doing. If there is concern that they are not being properly rewarded, additional pay reviews may be necessary, involving different staff or with a senior manager sitting in.

Work-related benefits

If you are providing your employees with benefits such as staff meals or trips away, you have an obligation to ensure that they are available on an equal basis. This means making sure that trans people will be welcome and will be treated with respect in the venues you choose. If you're not sure if a particular venue will be suitable, ask your trans employees what they think, but make sure they don't feel pressured to agree with your suggestions. You may also be able to get helpful advice from local trans organisations. Remember that if you make the wrong choice and a trans employee has a bad experience as a result, it's likely to bring down the mood for everybody else too. It's in everyone's interests to get it right.

Individual employee benefits and rewards can also present problems on occasion. Sometimes tickets to concerts or sporting events, for example, may be difficult for trans people to use with confidence. If you can't find something that's suitable for everyone, the key is to have a variety of rewards available. This helps account for issues that may be faced by other specific groups of employees, such as disabled people, and it also accounts for the fact that not everybody likes the same musicians or sports teams. Vouchers are often a good option because they offer an element of choice.

Trans employees' family members

Every now and then, employers need to get in touch with their employees' families. This could be because of an accident at work, because they are trying to find out what has happened to an employee who has not shown up as expected, or because the employee has been held up due to a work situation and is not in a position to call directly. Family members may also be mentioned in Christmas cards or be sent invitations to workplace events. Whatever your reason for contacting them, it's important that they are respected just as any other employee's family would be.

A significant proportion of trans people are rejected by their families or lose touch with individual family members as a result of prejudice. This means that it's wise not to make assumptions about a trans employee's home life. Don't assume, for example, that a young trans employee who is taken to hospital will want you to contact their parents. Trans people may need to list friends as emergency contacts if they have no family members to support them. Others, however, have happy family lives with partners and children, so don't assume that their stories are tragic.

It's worth noting that transition can leave some families with complex identities. For example, the wife of somebody who was living as a man when they married but has since transitioned to live as a woman may remain happy with the marriage but not think of herself as lesbian or bisexual. The children of a trans woman may continue to call her 'Daddy' and she may be comfortable with this because she doesn't want to complicate things for them and doesn't feel that the nature of their relationship has changed. However, this doesn't mean that she'll be happy for other people to refer to her using masculine terms. If this feels confusing, think about how the children of separated parents can end up choosing unexpected terms to refer to different members of a larger and more complicated family.

Chapter 7

Health and Safety at Work

Common health and safety issues facing trans people

Every workplace faces different issues when it comes to health and safety. If you have one or more trans employees, there will be some specific areas where problems may arise more frequently or to a greater degree. This shouldn't put you off hiring trans people, as health and safety needs attention where every employee is concerned and they can still be a positive force in the workplace. Being alert to these issues, however, means you can do a better job of tackling them, and even preventing problems from arising in the first place.

Workplace harassment

Harassment can occur in any workplace, no matter how hard you work to try to ensure that your staff get along with each other. Trans people are particularly vulnerable to it. Sometimes it takes the form of outright aggression but often it's subtler, consisting of repeated barbed comments or small acts deliberately designed to make the working day more difficult. Over time, these things can accumulate to cause severe stress.

Research carried out by Totaljobs in 2016[40] found that only 50 per cent of respondents said their workplaces had guidelines in place making it clear that discrimination against trans employees would not be tolerated, whilst 38 per cent said that they had been discriminated against by colleagues.

Employers are legally liable for protecting their trans employees from harassment and discrimination in the workplace. Showing that you have a clear policy for discouraging harassment and tackling it if it does occur can provide you with some protection if you are taken to court over this. Legally, harassment of trans people is defined by the Protection from Harassment Act 1997 and the Equality Act 2010. It includes any targeted behaviour that is sexual in nature or related to gender reassignment and violates the target's dignity or creates an intimidating, hostile, degrading, humiliating or offensive environment.[41, 42]

Examples of harassment can include:

- persistent misgendering or refusal to acknowledge that transition has occurred

- threatening to tell people to whom the trans person has not come out that they are trans

- sending offensive comments or images through email or messaging systems

- refusing to cooperate with the trans person in group project work because they are trans

- physical harassment such as shoving the trans person or trying to trip them up

- sexual harassment such as making obscene suggestions or unwanted touching.

It's important to note that the law sees harassment the same way regardless of whether or not it was intentional. This means, for example, that repeated transphobic jokes which were intended as friendly banter can still be considered an offence. It is the responsibility of the person making such jokes to think about what the effect might be. Like other employees, trans people do not have a responsibility to 'toughen up' or to try not to be offended.

SEXUAL HARASSMENT

Sexual harassment against trans people is, sadly, quite common. It can occur regardless of the sexual preferences of the harasser because the intent often has more to do with a desire for power than with sexual attraction. Although trans women are most vulnerable, it can also happen to trans men and non-binary people. Trans men may find it particularly difficult to report because identifying themselves as victims of sexual aggression makes them feel less masculine and makes dysphoria worse. This is less of a problem if there is a workplace policy on sexual harassment that shows a clear awareness that not all victims are female.

It is important not to assume that trans women can or should defend themselves from sexual harassment because they have lived as men. Many people simply freeze in this situation, and it's easy for anyone to feel disempowered and vulnerable in a workplace context, especially if the harasser is a superior. Furthermore, trans women who have been taking hormone treatment for some time are unlikely to be as strong as male colleagues and may not be able to defend themselves physically. Lacking strength that they used to have may make them less physically confident and therefore more vulnerable to all kinds of bullying.

Sexual harassment doesn't just mean assault, but can include things like unwanted sexual comments, inappropriate touching or sending pornographic images in email. Sometimes employees are unsure where it crosses the line and when they can report it. You should encourage them to report anything that makes them feel uncomfortable, and you should always listen respectfully, even if you think they might have misinterpreted the situation. Accusations should always be taken seriously because of the harm that this kind of behaviour can cause. Even if there is no inappropriate intention behind it, behaviour which causes another employee distress needs to stop.

Sometimes people defend their sexual harassment of trans people by saying that trans women have deliberately chosen to make themselves attractive to men, or that trans men need to toughen up because they've chosen to enter a masculine world in which certain things are just banter. Non-binary people are sometimes told that they're just looking for attention or that it's not the harasser's fault if they're confused. Obviously, attitudes like this are seriously out of line. Sexual harassment is never the fault of the victim. Anybody who uses arguments like this can be in no doubt that their behaviour is causing distress, and is doing it deliberately.

Sexual harassment is also a criminal offence. No employee should ever feel pressured to let it be dealt with purely as an internal company matter if they want to involve the police.

SEXIST BEHAVIOUR FROM COLLEAGUES

People transitioning from living as men to living as women sometimes find themselves on the receiving end of sexist behaviour, which they may be less confident about dealing with than women who have encountered it throughout their lives. Just like transphobia, sexism can have a damaging effect on mental health, but it can often go undetected if employers are looking out for transphobia instead, which may mean that the measures put in place to tackle harassment are not the most effective ones. The easiest way to deal with this is to make sure trans women are aware of the possibility before any problem can arise, and to make sure they know who they can talk to if it happens.

Because they are dealing with it for the first time, trans women can sometimes be more sensitive about sexist behaviour in the workplace than other female employees are. This does not mean, however, that those other employees are not bothered by it at all, or that it is not having a damaging effect on their performance. Instead of concluding that the trans employee needs to toughen up, an employer hearing concerns like this should consider the possibility that behaviour that has so far been taken for granted and treated as trivial could actually be harmful. Changing this kind of behaviour when it is ingrained in workplace culture can be challenging, but results in a workplace that is happier and healthier all round once the effort has been made.

IDENTIFYING HARASSMENT

It's important not to assume that victims of harassment will report what is happening to them. They may not be sure how to, or they may try to put up with it because they don't want to make a fuss, or they may worry that they won't be taken seriously. They could even be concerned that making a report could backfire on them. This is a particular problem for trans employees, who often feel, rightly or wrongly, that their employment situation is precarious and that they would struggle if they had to find another job. In that situation, they may be afraid of rocking the boat.

Situations can also occur in which an employee complains of harassment to their immediate manager but the manager does nothing and the complaint doesn't get escalated. This is why it's worth paying extra attention to situations in which employees are particularly vulnerable, such as when somebody has recently come out as trans or when a trans person has been moved between departments.

When a victim of harassment doesn't come forward, the problem can show up in other ways. A high absence rate, especially if absences relate to stress or minor illnesses, can be a warning sign. Sometimes other employees will be concerned about things they have witnessed. It's important that they know how to pass on their concerns to somebody who can investigate.

DEVELOPING AN ANTI-HARASSMENT POLICY

It's much easier to prevent harassment and bullying if you have a clear policy in place from the outset. A basic anti-harassment policy should include the following:

- a statement asserting the organisation's commitment to equality

- examples of unacceptable types of behaviour

- examples of how employees can help (e.g. by going to equality training)

- information on who to talk to about any instances of harassment

- reassurance that reporting harassment will never lead to the reporter being penalised.

Offering an anonymous reporting option can encourage reporting. It's difficult to use anonymous reports as evidence in a disciplinary process because they could themselves be intended to harass an unpopular employee, but they can still be useful in tipping you off to a possible problem, so that you know when to investigate.

Your anti-harassment policy should be proactively made available to employees. You could do this by advising them to read it at the point when they are hired, posting it on workplace noticeboards and reminding them of it during staff meetings. It should also be easy for employees to access in their own time (e.g. because it's available on the company website).

Your employees will only have confidence in your anti-harassment policy if it's clear that managers take it seriously and that breaches are dealt with promptly. Before formally launching a new policy, get your managers and HR team together to discuss in detail what it involves. Make sure that they all know their responsibilities and are also aware of whom they should go to if they need further guidance on implementation.

Stress at work

Even in the absence of other workplace problems, trans people can be more vulnerable to stress than other workers are. They are less likely to have a strong support network at home and are more likely to have experienced trauma. If they are not receiving adequate medical treatment, dysphoria can cause stress, and inconsistent hormone treatment can also be problematic. This doesn't mean they are less able to handle tough jobs – in fact, they may be more likely than other workers to have developed effective coping methods – but indicators of stress should be taken seriously and appropriate support offered.

Stress is a serious issue in any workplace. It is responsible for around 15 million working days being lost to the British economy every year. Left unresolved, it can lead to serious mental health problems such as depression or anxiety, and it also increases the risk of cardiovascular problems, stroke and several types of cancer. It is, however, easy to fix in most cases. Even if work issues are not at the root of the problem, a supportive work environment can make a big difference. It's important to let employees know that if they're suffering from stress then they can discuss it with their managers or HR personnel without their jobs being under threat as a result. This gives the employer a chance to help, reducing the risk of days being lost to ill-health and, often, increasing the employee's productivity. Supporting an employee like this also increases their loyalty to the organisation.

Capacity issues in manual occupations

Most people assume that, whatever else happens to her, a trans woman will retain the physical advantages that go with being born in a masculine body, and will be bigger and stronger than other women. In fact, this is not always the case. If she has been receiving hormonal treatment from before puberty, she will be no stronger than any other woman. If she transitions in adulthood, she will probably lose a significant amount of her muscle mass. In some cases the effect is dramatic.

Some trans women still work in manual occupations, just as other women do, but you shouldn't assume that they will be able to undertake all the same tasks as men – you will have to assess them individually. If you have an employee who is receiving hormone treatment to give her a more feminine body, you will need to reassess her roughly every three months in order to make sure you know what her safe limits are. Most people going through this process stabilise after two years, so from that point onwards you can put them through periodic assessments at the same intervals as you do for other employees.

Security issues

As an employer, you have a duty to ensure that your workplace is safe for everybody. In some types of workplace, routine searches are carried out in order to deter theft or corporate espionage. It is important to be sensitive in your approach to searches where trans people are concerned.

Trans women should always be searched by women and trans men should always be searched by men, regardless of whether or not they have had surgery. Normal search procedures should not involve contact with intimate areas of the body anyway. Staff conducting searches should not ask questions about surgery, as this can make the situation highly intimidating.

Because these situations involve direct physical contact, it is important that you also show sensitivity to those carrying them out. Some employees may feel unsafe carrying out such searches, a problem that can potentially be resolved by educating them further about trans issues. Others may feel that it conflicts with their religious principles, which is harder to resolve. In some cases you may simply need to bring in a different member of staff to carry out that search.

If you have a non-binary employee, you should ask them who they feel most comfortable being searched by.

Difficulty in organising appropriate searches should never lead to the trans employee being discriminated against, for example by being denied the opportunity for promotion because this would involve moving to a section of the workplace where searches are mandatory.

Chapter 8

Transgender People in Public-Facing Roles

Public responses to trans people: what to expect

Many employers worry about placing trans people in public-facing roles because they don't want to have to deal with negative reactions. Some worry that it could deter customers or create unnecessary tension. These concerns can present serious barriers to trans people looking for employment or trying to make the most of their talents in the workplace. The reality is that the rate of problems arising from having a trans person in a role like this varies by geographical location and industry sector. In nearly all cases it's less of a problem than employers expect, and in many cases there are no problems at all. This chapter provides advice on what to do when problems do arise, how you can calm public concerns and protect your employees, and what you can do to make such problems less likely to develop in the first place.

Employers should be aware that they are legally liable if their employees are harassed at work by customers.

This involves a 'three strikes' rule. If harassment has occurred on two previous occasions and you have not taken all reasonable steps to ensure that it can't happen again, you may then be charged if it happens a third time. This applies even if a different third party is involved on each occasion.

Proactive ways to protect your trans employees

The first thing you need when you're working out how to protect your employees is information. There are three ways to get this:

- Talk to professional organisations dedicated to supporting trans people or LGBTI people more generally.

- Talk to local trans or LGBTI support groups.

- Ask trans employees themselves for input on what problems they anticipate.

Several organisations exist to support trans people, or LGBTI people more generally, in relation to specific professions. Some are independent and others are sub-groups within larger organisations, such as trade unions and professional guilds. Most have a website or a social media presence, and many are run entirely through social media platforms so that they can achieve a national reach despite having relatively few members. They can be excellent sources of information on industry-specific issues (see the Further Information section at the end of this book).

Local support groups are very good when what you want is to know how accepted trans people are in your local area. Often they will agree to meet with you or they will talk to their members on your behalf and collect their stories about what it's like to deal with members of the public in a work capacity. They may also have useful suggestions to help things go more smoothly.

Your trans employees themselves will usually have some awareness of the issues they're likely to face, both in dealing with local people and in working in your particular sector. They will also be able to discuss their personal comfort levels and what they think they can and can't handle. Everybody is different in this regard, so don't assume that one trans person being comfortable with something means another is obliged to be comfortable as well. Stress the importance of being honest about any concerns and of reporting difficulties that develop after starting a particular type of work, because problems are always more easily dealt with if tackled early.

It's very important that your customers and other visitors to your workplace see your trans employees treated respectfully by their colleagues. This, together with having the correct name and gender on things like name badges, is important in providing cues about how it's appropriate to behave, and so reduces the risk of harassment.

The following sections describe a range of problems your trans employees may encounter in the workplace, including steps you can take to help prevent them happening in the first place and advice on how to deal with them if they do occur.

Telephone communications and voice issues

Many trans people are uncomfortable about the way their voices sound, especially if they are in the early stages of transition. People who take hormones to masculinise their bodies experience their voices breaking in the same way most boys do during their teenage years. This can be awkward and embarrassing when it's happening, but afterwards they will sound like other men. For trans women, however, the issue is more complicated. A voice that has broken can never fully return to its previous state, and even though surgery is available to help with this, it can be risky and it doesn't always produce impressive results. This means that many trans women are stuck with masculine-sounding voices. Over time, they can learn vocal tricks to make their voices softer, but many will always risk being mistaken for men because of the way they sound, and this is especially problematic on the phone where there are no other clues to a speaker's gender.

For this reason, many trans people are acutely uncomfortable about doing telephone work, especially early on in transition, before they have begun to gain control of how they sound. This means it's a good idea to discuss phone work with your trans employees and look for alternative ways of working where appropriate.

Dealing with prejudice

The law requires you to support any employee who is confronted with prejudice based on a protected characteristic, including employees who are confronted with transphobic prejudice. In a situation like this, you should politely but firmly make it clear that such behaviour is not acceptable. Most people expressing prejudice believe that they have the support of others, and they will usually back down quickly if you make it clear that you don't agree with them and that they, not your employee, are behaving inappropriately.

Harassing or threatening somebody because they are trans is a hate crime. It can be useful to point this out and to let the offender know if they have been caught on your security cameras – this can be a very effective deterrent and often leads to people apologising. In many cases, people expressing prejudice are unaware that their behaviour is criminal and don't even understand that they're being rude. Therefore, where possible, and if your employee is comfortable with it, you should give the offender the opportunity to apologise. Whether or not further action is warranted should always be up to the trans person because only they can know how they have been affected by the incident, but often an apology will provide the best resolution for all involved, especially if it's clear that it has led to somebody rethinking prejudice.

It's important not to be judgemental about how trans people react to incidents like this. Sometimes they may seem oversensitive, but if so it's usually because they have to deal with so many such incidents that the combined effect is highly stressful. Other trans people may be dismissive of prejudiced behaviour that seems shocking to you, because their response to encountering a lot of it has been to become thick-skinned. Either way, the important factor is that it's the trans person who will be most strongly impacted both by the incident and by the response to it, so the trans person must take a leading role in deciding what should be done.

In some cases trans people may not want incidents to go to court because they are not out to everybody in their lives (e.g. it's not uncommon for secrets to be kept from elderly relatives) and they're worried about being outed by media attention in relation to a court case.

If you need to call the police

If you encounter serious difficulty in persuading a member of the public who has harassed or threatened a trans employee to leave your premises, or if you suspect that they are loitering outside with the intention of causing trouble, you may need to call the police. Most larger police stations have an LGBT liaison officer who is specially trained in understanding the kind of hostility faced by trans people, and who will be able to interview your trans employee in a suitably sensitive way. An officer like this will be best placed to determine if a hate crime has been committed. If they are not immediately available, you can still request that they be alerted to the case in order to be sure that it's handled as well as possible.

Preventing future incidents

The law requires that when one of your employees has had to deal with transphobic prejudice, you take action to ensure that they are not in that situation again. Of course, anybody can be unlucky, and if an incident occurs that you could not reasonably have foreseen, you are not likely to find yourself in trouble as a result. What the authorities will want to see is evidence that you have taken all reasonable steps within your power to keep your employee safe.

With this in mind, should you remove your trans employees from public-facing roles? That's actually up to the employees. If you offer an employee who has been harassed by a member of the public another role, with no drop in salary or status, and they decide that they would rather remain where they are, you will be seen to have acted reasonably (though you may still be required to take other reasonable steps, such as making sure that they have the correct name badge). The law does not oblige you to prevent your employees from taking risks of this sort if they wish to do so, as long as they don't feel forced to do so and as long as you support them if and when problems occur.

In many cases, the best way to avoid future incidents is to discuss what happened with your employee and ask if there is any action you could take that they feel would make them safer.

The *Employment Statutory Code of Practice*[43] suggests taking the following steps:

- Have a policy on harassment.

- Notify third parties that harassment of employees is unlawful and will not be tolerated (e.g. by displaying a public notice).

- Include a term in all contracts with third parties notifying them of your policy on harassment and requiring them to adhere to it.

- Encourage employees to report any acts of harassment by third parties, to enable you to support the employee and take appropriate action.

- Take action on every complaint of harassment by a third party.

Conferences, events and trade shows

As well as dealing with customers, your trans employees may sometimes be dealing with people from outside your organisation when they attend conferences, events or trade shows. Every employee wants to make a good impression when representing the company in this kind of role, so it's important that they know that this doesn't mean they're obliged to put up with discrimination or prejudiced remarks. If you can't be there to stand up for your employees, you need to empower them as much as possible to stand up for themselves.

In a situation like this, the event organisers are responsible for making sure that no discrimination occurs. If your employee has any complaints about them failing to do this, you should be ready to step in and challenge them about it. When you are running events yourself, you should be ready to defend the rights of other trans people who may be present, as well as your own employees, and you should expect organisations playing host to your employees to take the same approach.

Increasingly, trans people report that they are participating in events like this without problems. You shouldn't be hesitant about letting your trans employees represent your company if they feel confident about doing so.

Secondments and on-site placements

If you routinely arrange secondments or on-site placements for your employees, you will need to be certain that the places they are going to are suitable for them and that they will not be on the receiving end of harassment or discrimination there. This is particularly important if these placements are mandatory in your organisation or if they are linked to opportunities for promotion.

Despite these potential issues, many trans people welcome the chance to spend time in different working environments, learning new skills and gaining important experience. If you anticipate challenges in a particular place, discuss them with the individual employee concerned and let them be part of the process of working out what to do. Work with your counterparts in the new location, discuss their equality and diversity policies and ask what assurances they can give you. Make sure that you show full confidence in your employee's abilities. Successful placements like this can help new firms learn to respect trans people and improve the chances of them making trans employees welcome within their own organisations.

If you are seconding people overseas, you can find further information in Chapter 10.

Can trans employees make your business more approachable?

People in minority groups are often cautious about who they do business with because they don't know where they might encounter prejudice. If it's clear that there are trans people working for your company, this can help to put other people at ease. Because trans people tend to be more visible than gay, lesbian and bisexual people, and because people and organisations that are accepting of trans people tend to be accepting of all LGBT people, this is a particularly good way to reach this market segment.

If you have trans staff but they are not visible, either because they blend in easily or they don't happen to be in public-facing roles, they may still be able to help you because they will often be able to advise on what makes them feel happier about approaching a company. Their personal expertise can help you to improve customer relations, and can also help you to broaden the pool of candidates available to you next time you start a recruitment drive.

Public attitudes towards trans people are most positive among the young, and showing that your company has a positive attitude to diversity can improve your reputation among potential customers in their teens and twenties. It helps you seem up-to-date and forward-looking.

Chapter 9

Medical Issues and Time Off Work

Specific health issues affecting trans people

It is illegal to discriminate against a trans employee because they need time off for medical procedures relating to transition. Employers should treat this kind of time off in the same way they would if any other employee needed time off for medical reasons. But how much time off is likely to be needed by somebody going through transition, and what other issues should employers be aware of?

Transition and surgery: what to expect

Contrary to popular belief, there is no one-size-fits-all surgical process that trans people go through. As part of the transition process, they may undergo a number of different procedures, sometimes years apart.

Trans men may undergo one or more of the following surgical procedures:

- ovary removal

- hysterectomy

- breast removal

- scrotal construction

- phallic construction

- facial reconstruction.

Trans women may undergo one or more of the following surgical procedures:

- testicle removal

- genital reconstruction

- breast enhancement

- facial reconstruction

- vocal surgery.

Among trans people, the term *top surgery* is routinely used to describe surgical procedures on the chest, whilst *bottom surgery* is used to describe surgical procedures on the genitals or reproductive organs. Using these terms can be a handy way of discussing the subject without embarrassment.

With the exception of scrotal construction, which is a comparatively minor procedure, genital reconstruction surgeries are lengthy procedures which require the patient to be in good health beforehand and which can take some time to recover from. When facing any lengthy surgical procedure, patients are advised to stop taking hormones for several weeks beforehand in order to avoid an associated risk of blood clots – this advice also applies in more commonplace circumstances, with women taking contraceptive pills also advised to stop in the run-up to operations. For trans people, having to go without hormones can be very unsettling. It can lead to mood swings, depression and general feelings of exhaustion. If you know that one of your employees is intending to undergo surgery like this in the near future, it's a good idea to discuss how this difficult time can best be approached. Most people don't want to take time off work because work itself can help them to cope, but they may find it easier to handle some types of task than others. As soon as they are able to return to their usual hormone treatment regime, they will be themselves again, with no lasting ill-effects.

Facial reconstruction surgery is generally only available privately. It can be very expensive and trans people who choose to undergo it often travel abroad in order to save money, avoid waiting lists or visit the surgeons with the best reputations. Although it might sound like a luxury, it can have a big effect on a trans person's quality of life as it can make it much easier for them to be accepted in their new gender role and get on with life without having to deal with prejudice or discrimination.

Vocal surgery, designed to feminise the voice, can be carried out in a variety of ways. One of the most popular methods is the tracheal shave, which reduces the size of the Adam's apple as well as raising the pitch of the voice. When it works well, the results of this surgery can be very impressive, but if it goes wrong it can leave people with unnaturally high voices or make it hard for them to speak at all. It is therefore a good idea to discuss this procedure if an employee brings it up and is comfortable doing so, in order to work out how situations like that could be managed in the workplace.

An increasingly popular alternative to the tracheal shave is vocal fold shortening, which doesn't change the appearance of the neck but is a safer way to raise the pitch of the voice. This doesn't carry the same risks as a tracheal shave although it does require significant healing time, with patients usually advised not to speak at all for a month and to be careful for some time after that. Generally, people who have undergone this procedure will still be well enough in every other way to re-enter the workplace, but obviously adjustments will have to be made, not just to keep them away from work that requires speaking but also to find alternative ways for them to communicate with colleagues. One solution is for them to carry a smartphone or tablet on which they can quickly type what they wish to say.

Trans men do not undergo vocal surgery but usually experience some natural deepening of the voice within a few months of starting to take testosterone. This is not usually problematic but can occasionally result in a day or two of difficulty speaking, which is essentially the same thing that many boys go through during adolescence. An alternative approach to taking testosterone, or if testosterone has not achieved the desired effect, is for trans men to work with voice coaches – the same people who help actors and politicians – in order to learn how to pitch their voices in a way they feel more comfortable with.

Recuperation issues after surgery

With any surgical procedure, the amount of time needed for recovery is closely related to whether or not a general anaesthetic is required and, if so, how long the patient needs to be under anaesthesia. When it comes to transition, the biggest issue is genital surgery. Because it can require several hours of general anaesthetic, patients may need as long as 12 weeks to recover.

Facial surgery, by contrast, does not now require the patient to be unconscious for long, and may only necessitate 1–2 days in hospital for observation. Patients are generally forbidden to drive for 2–3 weeks, but can otherwise return to their day-to-day activities within a few days. Bruising, however, can last for several weeks, and there can also be facial numbness, which makes it hard for patients to feel confident that their faces are moving as intended. If you've tried to smile at somebody after having a dental anaesthetic and have found you're uncertain about whether you're grimacing instead, you'll know what this feels like. Accordingly, you should be sensitive to the possibility that a trans person who has recently had facial surgery might prefer to avoid public-facing work for a month or two.

Hysterectomy and removal of ovaries or testicles are relatively commonplace operations performed for all sorts of health reasons. Because of this, surgical techniques are advanced and they can be performed relatively quickly, which means that patients are usually fit to return to work within a week to ten days. Because the latter two procedures stop the body from producing the wrong sort of hormones, trans people who undergo them will often feel a lot better, and be more productive, once they have been done.

Surgery on the breasts, whether to remove or enhance them, can now be done on an outpatient basis, provided that the patient is in good health. A general anaesthetic may not be needed, with local anaesthetic and sedation often being a practical alternative. This means that a trans person undergoing this process may not need more than a couple of days off work. Individual experiences vary because whilst some people are fine, others suffer from a lot of associated pain. You should therefore be alert to the fact that recovery could take longer although this no longer constitutes a major operation.

Trans people on hormone treatment

Today it is normal for trans people to start supervised hormone treatment as soon as they get a firm diagnosis from a specialist. Because waiting to see a specialist can take some time, however, some trans people acquire hormones from other sources in the meantime. Unsupervised hormone treatment carries the same risks as any medication acquired on the black market (such as diet pills or steroids used for muscle gain). The most common problem is with inconsistent dosage, which can cause emotional problems and feelings of physical exhaustion. Because professional support is usually just a few months away, this is unlikely to cause more problems than common afflictions such as insomnia or a persistent cold. If you have concerns, talk to your employee to see if there are more effective ways to manage the workload in the short term, such as rearranging shift patterns or changing the type of tasks they are required to undertake.

Mood swings and tiredness can be an issue for trans women during the first 3–4 months of professionally supervised hormone treatment, just as they are for many non-trans women who start using contraceptive pills. In most cases this is not severe, but it can make people who are already in a vulnerable situation, going through a transition at work, feel more emotionally sensitive. This makes it all the more important that employers offer adequate support. These issues normally diminish as the body gets used to its new hormone balance.

Trans people on hormone therapy need to be monitored on an ongoing basis to make sure they don't have blood-pressure problems, which are a risk for anyone whose hormonal balance goes awry. This may sometimes mean that they need time off work for check-ups, though the increasing use of home monitors for blood pressure, together with the availability of drop-in testing services at pharmacies, is reducing this need.

Trans women and facial hair removal

Although women capable of growing beards are a lot more common than you might think, we tend to think of facial and body hair as a masculine characteristic. For trans women who already risk being misidentified as male or taunted about masculine aspects of their appearance, 'excess' hair can be particularly distressing. Hormone treatment and the removal of testicles generally reduces hair growth but doesn't always stop it. This means that many trans women need to undergo laser hair removal if they want to resolve the problem.

The laser hair-removal process requires multiple appointments, though individually they don't take very long so a considerate employer should not have too much difficulty amending work schedules to fit around them. They can, however, cause other issues. First, they are painful and leave parts of the face inflamed, like bad sunburn, so employees should ideally not have to deal with the public immediately after returning from them; they may also need multiple short breaks to apply pain-relieving cream. Second, before a laser session can commence, stubble has to be present on the face – ideally two or more days' growth. This can be acutely embarrassing for a trans woman, so, again, it's best to offer her work that doesn't involve dealing with strangers if this is possible. Employers will need to be ready to step in if other employees make fun, as they may not understand what is going on. Some trans women opt to wear heavy make-up at this time in an effort to conceal stubble, and this should not be treated as a violation of dress codes.

Other health issues

After taking hormones for two years, a trans man will face most of the same general health risks as any other man, and a trans woman will face the same general health risks as other women. There are a few notable exceptions to this rule. Trans women do not face the same risk of breast cancer as other women (scientists have yet to work out why). They continue to face a risk of prostate cancer, and although this is much lower than that faced by men, they need to get check-ups to stay safe as they get older.

Occasionally, trans men can have problems because their dose of testosterone is set too high, leading to issues with cholesterol, high blood pressure and cardiovascular problems (also a risk for men who produce unusually high levels of testosterone by themselves). However, as long as they are regularly having check-ups, these problems can usually be identified and the dose adjusted before serious medical issues develop.

Hormone use by trans women means that they may face a slightly higher than average risk of cardiovascular problems and stroke, equivalent to that of non-trans women using the contraceptive pill over the age of 40, but this risk can be reduced with exercise and a healthy diet. Trans men using hormones face a slightly higher than average risk of liver problems, but can reduce this by eating sensibly and avoiding heavy alcohol use. In short, being trans presents less of a risk to a person's health than smoking, heavy drinking or simple inactivity.

Mental health issues

The Diagnostic and Statistical Manual of Mental Disorders (*DSM*), which is published by the American Psychiatric Association (APA) and used as a reference guide worldwide, used to classify being transgender as a mental illness in itself, but no longer does so. This reflects a change in thinking about the nature of gender identity, how it is situated in the brain, and how dysphoria can be treated, with the weight of scientific evidence now showing clearly that 'reparative therapy' – designed to make people feel comfortable in the gender categories they were placed in at birth – doesn't work.

Although gender dysphoria is now seen as a medical issue which can be treated with hormone therapy and surgery, the APA and other major psychiatric organisations note that trans people face a higher than average risk of certain other mental health problems, particularly depression and anxiety. Most experts think that this is a result of having to deal with other people's prejudice and with discrimination. This means that although, on average, trans people are more likely to be mentally ill, providing a supportive workplace environment can decrease the risk they face. Financial insecurity and discrimination in employment are understood to be major contributors to these types of mental illness generally, so employers should not underestimate the contribution they can make by getting things right.

Health insurance

Private health insurance companies do not normally offer gender confirmation surgery as standard, and some offer no support for treating gender dysphoria at all. Any employer wishing to provide cover of this type has to purchase it as an add-on.

In May 2016, Lloyds Bank became the first employer in the United Kingdom to offer gender confirmation surgery as part of its general health insurance cover for employees.[44] It estimated that only 0.025 per cent of its total workforce – 2.4 per cent of its openly trans workforce – would seek to use this facility but felt that having it in place was important to its aim to be an inclusive employer, would help to promote its brand and could help it to attract high-calibre LGBT graduates, thus providing several material benefits to the company as well as to the employees directly affected.

For employers already offering health insurance as an employee benefit, including gender confirmation surgery has other potential benefits. Sending a clear signal about the company's attitude to diversity increases the likelihood that trans employees and lesbian, gay and bisexual employees will come out, decreases their stress and potentially increases their productivity, as well as helping to create a more open and positive office culture. It also means that employees with gender dysphoria are likely to be able to access treatment much more quickly than they can on the NHS, thereby reducing their risk of mental health problems and stress-related physical health problems; and enabling any necessary medical procedures to be carried out in a way that fits around the person's other commitments, including work. This makes it much easier to organise cover during time off work and to make sure that the right support is in place at different stages in the process.

Chapter 10

Transgender People Working Internationally

Legal and cultural issues facing trans people internationally

Despite the challenges they still face, trans people in the United Kingdom today are much better protected legally and more socially accepted than they were in decades past. Unfortunately, the same is not true everywhere in the world. If your normal business practice involves foreign travel, what do you need to know in order to make sure your trans employees are safe and able to do their jobs effectively?

International attitudes to trans people vary enormously. In some places there are legal obstacles that make it difficult for trans people to visit the country at all. In others, social attitudes create a safety risk. Travel itself can be complicated by the attitudes of border security staff. Despite this, many trans people travel successfully in the course of their work. The important thing is that you understand the issues, know how to stay up to date, and work with your employees to find solutions to problems wherever possible.

Travel within Europe

There is no country remaining in Europe where it is illegal to be trans, and many European countries have anti-discrimination laws protecting trans people. This makes Europe the easiest continent for trans people to do business in. Cultural attitudes vary and, as a rule, trans people are more likely to meet with hostility in the east or in rural areas. Major cities are generally as safe as anywhere in the United Kingdom. It's still a good idea for your employee to contact local trans groups, however, in order to get advice on any particular areas to avoid or issues to be aware of.

Countries where being trans is illegal

Laws effectively making it illegal to be trans usually focus on cross-dressing, since they don't recognise the concept of a gender identity that might be different from physical sex. This means that a trans person who has undergone surgery on both the upper and lower body and has identity documents which match their gender may be safe as far as the law is concerned, but is still likely to be at risk of arrest unless able to blend in physically so that no suspicion is aroused.

In 2014, a Malaysian court ruled that Malaysia's law against cross-dressing was unconstitutional,[45] but the country persisted in arresting and convicting people under the law. Because it is derived from Sharia, this law applies only to Muslims (including people who were raised as Muslim but no longer identify that way).

In North Korea, it's illegal for men to have long hair and for women to wear trousers. Because visitors there are always considered to face some risk, it is strongly advised that people only visit if they are able to conform to these rules. Sudan also outlaws trousers on women and has, in the past, arrested men for wearing make-up, even though they were doing so in a professional context as models in a fashion show.[46]

In some other countries there are no specific laws making it criminal to be trans, but trans people are poorly understood and may face harassment or even arrest at the hands of law-enforcement officials who perceive them to be gay, where gay sexual activity (sometimes as minor as kissing) is illegal. Mauritania and Yemen fall into this category – in both countries, gay sex between men can result in the death penalty, and being trans is routinely confused with being gay. (Gay sex can also result in the death penalty in Iran, but trans people are recognised there as something different and are treated with some sympathy by the authorities in urban areas.) The death penalty also applies in some economically powerful countries, such as Nigeria, Singapore and Egypt.

In some other countries, there are no laws prohibiting being either trans or gay, but police harassment of people in these groups is common. This is the case in, for example, Uganda and Russia.

Other laws affecting trans people

In most parts of the world it is not illegal simply to be trans, and trans people can travel and do business in relative safety. Even in these countries, however, local laws can complicate how trans people undertake daily activities. For example, in parts of the United States there are laws which make it illegal for anyone to use public toilet facilities that do not correspond to their birth gender. This creates a particular risk for trans women, who risk arrest (or vigilante action) if they use female facilities but are at risk of sexual violence, like other women, if they use male ones. This type of situation means that it's important to check the legal situation before you send a trans employee abroad, and make sure you are able to alert them to issues of this sort.

Saudi Arabia has no actual laws on trans people but has a history of acting aggressively to prohibit people it identifies as men from wearing make-up and 'behaving like women'. It has shown in the past that it is as willing to apply this approach to foreign visitors as well as to its own citizens. According to Human Rights Watch, punishments have included imprisonment and flogging.

Countries with a high rate of transphobic crimes

In some countries, even where it is not illegal to be trans, trans people face a high level of violence and should exercise caution about how they move around and where they go. Brazil is currently considered to be the most dangerous country in this regard, with a high rate of transphobic murders in recent years, despite the fact that 50 per cent of Brazilians say they personally know a trans person – the highest rate in the world. Peru and Jamaica are also high-risk areas. The Foreign Office can provide up-to-date advice about the risk level in different countries.

Cultural attitudes to trans people

Some countries, such as India and Thailand, have long-established traditions of recognising third-genders, in addition to male and female. This should not, however, be interpreted as meaning that there is no discrimination against trans people there. Often such groups are restricted to particular social roles and it's difficult for trans people native to those countries to get jobs that don't fit with those roles. They may be treated respectfully when they conform but be unwelcome in professional environments. In these countries, however, allowances are usually made for foreigners, and British people travelling to these countries can expect to be treated with courtesy in most situations.

In some countries, such as Samoa, trans people are seen in a positive light and visitors may find that they have fewer problems than they do at home. Spain, Sweden, Canada and Germany have the highest rates of overall acceptance of trans people.[47]

It's important to note that cultural understandings of trans people vary. There is a host of different terms used internationally for people who have genders which are not male or female, and for people who move between genders, but they don't tend to map precisely onto the Western concept of a trans person. Sometimes they include intersex people, even though in the West most intersex people have a male or female gender. This means that, although it can be useful to know the terms that come closest to meaning *transgender* in the country your employee is travelling to, you should be aware that they are unlikely to be an exact match, and this could potentially cause confusion. The existence of additional recognised genders can also be problematic when trans people simply want to be recognised as male or female, as people from some cultural backgrounds can find it difficult to understand why they're not happy being placed in another category. This shouldn't create serious problems in a professional context but it's helpful to be aware of it.

Access to medication

Even if a trans person is able to visit a particular country for work, they may not be able to take their medication with them or get it prescribed in that country. If they are not using hormones or the trip will only take 24 hours, this may not be a problem. In some cases, trans men may be able to travel for a longer period because they receive their hormones through periodic injections rather than taking them orally on a daily basis. Coming off hormones is very difficult for trans people and in some instances it can cause serious health problems, so it is not acceptable to ask a trans person to do this.

If there are issues with medication and your trans employee remains keen to make the visit, they should speak to a doctor to find out if any alternative medication may be available in that country. You should both accept that, if this is not the case, the visit may not be possible.

How to help your trans employees travel more easily

The Foreign Office provides up-to-date travel advice for every country, which includes cautionary information for trans people. It is always a good idea to consult this before making decisions about where you can safely send your trans employees. It can also be helpful to contact a local trans support group to ask what problems, if any, they would anticipate.

You should never ask a trans employee to pretend not to be trans in order to do work in another country. Some trans employees may themselves suggest this, but if so, you should discuss the fact that there are risks attached. Somebody who is 'outed' and is believed to have concealed their transness may face greater hostility that somebody who has been open about it from the start. Sometimes a trans person may suggest trying to 'pass' in their old gender role, but in countries which are hostile to trans people, a man who seems a bit too feminine or a woman who seems a bit too masculine can also be at risk, and it can be very difficult to avoid giving off signals like this subconsciously.

Bear in mind that some trans people are determined not to miss out on opportunities because of their personal circumstances. Rather than ruling out travel that seems risky, you should discuss it with them, but be careful to ensure that they never feel they are under any pressure to put themselves at risk. You should always state explicitly that they won't be penalised for turning down such an assignment.

Working with your counterparts abroad

Even when there is a lot of hostility towards trans people in a particular country, you should not assume that the people you are doing business with will share that attitude. Generally speaking, more educated people are less likely to be prejudiced, and many professional people are willing to set aside their personal feelings in order to maintain a good business image and extend proper courtesy. They may find this easier to do when dealing with foreigners than they would when dealing with people who share their cultural background, because they can accept that your customs are different from theirs.

If your trans employee does not wish to hide their transness, or is unable to do so, you should ask if they are comfortable with you raising it with your counterparts abroad before the trip takes place. Where this is possible, it means that any misgivings can be dealt with ahead of time. It also makes it easier to ensure that practical arrangements are in place to minimise additional risks, so that transport, accommodation and hospitality arrangements do not present a problem.

What to do if a trans employee can't safely visit a country where work is being done

Sometimes you may be faced with a dilemma: your trans employee is clearly the best person for the job at hand, but you can't safely send them to the place where it needs to be done. In this situation it's possible to draw on accumulated best practice from similar situations affecting other groups. For example, there is a long history of women facing difficulties when travelling on business, due to legal and cultural issues and simple prejudice. These difficulties also affect some disabled people, and other people are unable to travel for health reasons; however, in many cases, they still manage to do their jobs.

Telecommuting may not be quite as good as face-to-face contact for building business relationships, but as more and more businesses adapt and get used to using it, the psychological barriers associated with it are falling away. When the work that needs to be done is centred on discussion and the exchange of ideas, it can be a very effective way of doing business – and it's also a lot cheaper than paying for transport and accommodation.

Some kinds of work that require physical engagement can also be undertaken through an adapted approach to telecommuting. It's now relatively easy to attach a small camera to a helmet, or use a tool like Google Glass, so that a person in a remote location can see what another is seeing. If the work involved is technical, such as checking on the progress of a construction project, it's useful if the person on site also has some level of technical expertise. You can send out another member of your team to do this or, for example, hire a postgraduate student from the appropriate department in a local university. This can enable your trans employee to work in partnership, remotely directing the person on site to make the observations that they need. Even surgeons now manage to work using this kind of teamwork.

In many situations, it makes sense simply to bring the people you're working with over to Britain and conduct business here, making sure that your hospitality is impressive enough to make up for any inconvenience.

Getting around

Because the process of transition can take quite some time, especially at a bureaucratic level, situations sometimes arise in which trans people needing to travel look male but have passports that say they are female, or vice versa. There is nothing illegal about travelling on a passport like this but it can create issues at security checkpoints, especially in airports, where the use of body scanners can also create problems for trans people who have amended their passports but have not had surgery. In order to reduce the risk of delays and intrusive search procedures, it's useful for your trans employees to be able to supply security staff with a number where you can be contacted (possibly outside office hours) to confirm the details of their travel arrangements and make it clear that they are who they say they are.

Foreign travel and promotion

In some companies, making work trips abroad is mandatory before employees can be considered for promotion. This can be discriminatory as far as trans people are concerned if they have fewer opportunities to work abroad – or none at all – because of the situation in the countries where work is being done. If this is the case, it's important to find a way to work around this, for example by simply dropping the requirement where trans employees are concerned (treating employees differently in this way is acceptable because although it means you're not treating everyone equally, you are treating everyone fairly – see the section on equality and fairness in Chapter 2). Whilst this is simple enough where promotion opportunities are being handled entirely by individuals, it can be problematic when part of the process is managed through computer systems. If this is the case, you will need to talk to your systems administrator about your options.

Encouraging good practice

Whether you are working abroad or within the United Kingdom, there are certain things you can do to help support trans people within other organisations as well as your own. This is an approach increasingly being adopted by major companies, and it can do a lot to improve the well-being of trans people across society as well as boosting your company's reputation.

Often the most significant factor in advancing human rights is one-to-one communication. Simply standing up for your trans employees in conversation, and challenging mistaken beliefs that other business people may have about what it means to be trans, can make a big difference. Even if it doesn't change minds straightaway, it can be the start of a learning process. Where you encounter other business people who want to do better in this area, you can exchange ideas and examples of best practice.

By working together with other organisations which share their concerns, businesses can sometimes make a difference to public policy. For example, the policies and policy statements of big companies like Target, PayPal and Deutsche Bank have encouraged several US states to throw out discriminatory legislation on toilet access for trans people, or to actively institute anti-discrimination legislation.

Other businesses can be encouraged to improve their practices when they are offered financial incentives for doing so. For example, you could offer preferential rates or priority bidding to companies with properly instituted equality policies which include protection for trans people.

As your experience with trans employees increases your personal knowledge base, you can contribute your knowledge to the wider community through trade organisations and local, national or international governmental organisations working with businesses. This is another great way to spread examples of best practice and reassure other business people, wherever they are in the world, that the challenges of taking on trans employees are not overwhelming and that trans people can be a positive asset in the workplace.

Chapter 11

The Benefits of Employing Transgender People

Trans people in the workplace

If this book has left you thinking that bringing trans people into your workplace could present a lot of challenges, it's worth bearing in mind that it can also bring a lot of benefits. Individual trans people can have impressive skills, experience and qualifications, just like anyone else, and they can also benefit you as an employer in several ways that you may not have considered.

Using individual strengths

Every trans person has different individual skills and talents, but there are also some qualities you are more likely to find in trans people than in the general population because of what they have learned as a result of dealing with the particular problems they face in life. They are likely to be strong-willed and good at getting results even in adverse circumstances, including those which require hard work over a prolonged period of time. They are likely to be good problem-solvers and skilled at thinking outside the box because of their experience in having to deal repeatedly with systems that don't fit their needs. They are also likely to be good negotiators because they will have had to win over hostile people and educate people confused by the issues they face in their personal lives. All these qualities can be very useful to an employer.

Personal strengths developed in this way may never have been applied in the workplace. It's up to you to help employees in this situation discover what they're capable of. This will benefit you as an employer and is also likely to increase the employees' confidence and boost their loyalty to your organisation.

Unveiling hidden sexism in the workplace

One of the interesting things about the increasing number of people transitioning in recent years, and the increasing acceptance of trans people in the workplace, is that it has begun to reveal hidden differences in the way male and female employees are treated. In a large workplace, discrimination is often difficult to spot, and it can be masked by the achievements of a few successful women. The experiences of trans people can be very helpful in identifying problems and finding solutions.

Kristen Schildt, a sociologist and author of the book *Just One of the Guys? Transgender Men and the Persistence of Gender Inequality*,[48] interviewed numerous trans men in the course of her research and found that they felt, overall, that they were taken more seriously post-transition and that, if they had previously been criticised for being aggressive, they were subsequently praised for being assertive. Paying close attention when an employee transitions can reveal these subtle differences in attitude that can affect women's promotion prospects and keep companies from taking full advantage of their abilities.

Being a visible presence

Because many trans people are visibly distinctive, they immediately send a message to people visiting the workplace, making it clear that you are an equal opportunities employer and put your principles into practice. This can, in turn, encourage members of other minority groups to apply for jobs with you, increasing the talent pool you have to draw on. It can give gay, lesbian and bisexual people in your workforce the confidence to come out, reducing their day-to-day stress levels and potentially increasing their productivity.

Providing a learning opportunity

Although no individual trans person should be expected to educate those around them and answer whatever questions they may be asked, personal or otherwise, simply getting used to the presence of a trans person in the workplace can have a positive effect on employees. It may encourage them to attend diversity training or learn more about trans people from books or the Internet. It may also have an impact because it dispels myths about trans people, making it clear that they're not so different from anyone else.

Getting used to trans people means that your employees will be far less likely to run into difficulties when dealing with trans customers or clients, or with trans people from other companies. With more and more trans people now feeling able to live openly, this is becoming increasingly important.

Financial benefits of diversity

Although no studies have been done into the financial impact of including trans employees in the workplace, there is evidence to show that diversity in general helps businesses to be more successful. A study[49] carried out in the United Kingdom, the United States and India in 2015 found that companies with at least one woman on the board significantly outperformed those run entirely by men. The UK study found that this represented an overall opportunity cost of US$74bn, or £59bn.

Why would this happen? There are several theories, and it may be that they all pay a part:

- Businesses that are open to employing and promoting a wider range of people have larger talent pools to draw from.

- People with different life experiences think differently, increasing the range of ideas available within the business.

- People who are well educated find prejudice disturbing and are more enthusiastic about working for companies that clearly value diversity.

- The general population is diverse, and companies that reflect this can more effectively reach out to potential customers from every part of the population.

Top companies are increasingly getting wise to the fact that diversity is good for business. An estimated 66 per cent of Fortune 500 companies now have anti-discrimination policies to protect trans employees.[50]

Feeding back

Often people who have gone through a successful transition at work, with the support of their employers, go on to feed back into the way that trans issues and diversity issues more widely are handled. They may be able to help develop new strategies so that the next trans person to come out in the workplace finds it easier, design information leaflets for other employees, help refine the company's mission statement in relation to diversity and provide training to other members of staff. They may also be willing to act as a point of contact for any future employees who come out as trans, so that there will be somebody available who not only knows the company's procedure for dealing with such situations but can directly relate to what the newly 'open' person is going through.

Stella, who works in environmental transport, rewrote her company's policy after transitioning at work. The old one had asked that people coming out as trans provide a Gender Recognition Certificate, which is very difficult for many trans people (as Chapter 3 makes clear), so she removed that section. She updated the language used and worked on streamlining the whole process, because one of the problems she'd faced was that whenever she needed anything done she had to go to a different set of people, forcing her to out herself repeatedly without knowing what the reaction might be. She hopes that the new policy will be more straightforward for the employer whilst making things much easier for trans employees.

Joe, who works as a counsellor, delivered an LGBT awareness course on behalf of Victim Support. He says that he found it difficult to do this without outing himself, but tried to avoid doing so at the start of the sessions he ran because he found that then the people who really needed to hear things would just switch off. When one training participant told him she would always know if somebody was trans, he told her that was interesting and came out to her. He says:

> Her jaw was on the floor. She said, 'Well that told me, didn't it?' It was quite powerful for the group.

Glossary

Terms

Acquired gender A gender role taken on after transition.

Agender A person who does not have a gender or cannot relate to the concept of gender.

Androgyne A person who is in between male and female or has elements of both, either mentally, bodily or in presentation.

Androgynous Having aspects of both male and female, or being in between male and female, either mentally, bodily or in presentation (e.g. clothing choices).

Bigender A term describing people whose gender has both male and female aspects, either sequentially or at the same time.

Binary transition Moving from male to female or from female to male.

Bottom surgery Transition-related surgery carried out on the genitals or reproductive organs.

Cisgender Having the gender that is usually expected of somebody assigned to a particular sex category at birth; the opposite of *transgender*.

Cis A short form of the word *cisgender*.

Cross-dressing The term used when a man wears clothes normally associated with women, or (rarely) a woman wears clothes normally associated with men.

Deadname A name associated with a previous gender role, which a trans person no longer uses.

Deadnaming Using a name associated with a trans person's previous gender role, often with malicious intent.

Dysphoria A sense of unease, dissatisfaction and distress. In trans people, this often stems from a disparity between their sense of gender and the way their bodies look or are perceived by other people.

Equality Act A piece of legislation passed by the UK government in 2010 with the aim of providing protection from discrimination for a number of specific groups, including trans people who have transitioned or intend to transition, people mistaken for them and people associated with them.

FTM Female to male – person who has transitioned, is transitioning or intends to transition from a female gender role to a male gender role.

Gender binary A view of gender as consisting of just male and female.

Gender confirmation surgery Surgery carried out on the genitals to make them more like what would be expected of a person of the patient's gender (e.g. the creation of a vagina for a trans woman).

Gender fluid A term which refers to a sense of personal gender that fluctuates. It is used to describe somebody who feels more masculine at certain times and more feminine at others, and who may adopt different forms of gender presentation in accordance with this.

Gender identity An individual's sense of their own gender, whether male, female or something else.

Gender non-conforming A term describing a person whose expression of gender does not fit most people's expectations.

Gender presentation How a person communicates gender, involving things like clothing choice, deliberate pitching of the voice higher or lower, and social behaviour.

Gender queer A person whose relationship with gender is unconventional and who does not identify as male or female.

Gender questioning A term describing a person who is going through the process of exploring gender and understanding their own identity in gendered terms.

Gender reassignment The process of moving from one gender role to another. This term is usually used to refer to either a medical process or a legal process (or both).

Gender Recognition Act A piece of legislation passed by the UK government in 2004, designed to recognise a change of sex designation in law and provide trans people with most of the same rights as other people in relation to their gender.

Gender Recognition Certificate (GRC) A certificate issued according to the provisions of the Gender Recognition Act, entitling an individual to recognition of their maleness or femaleness for most legal purposes.

Gender spectrum A view of gender as existing on a spectrum from maleness or masculinity to femaleness or femininity, with other genders in between.

Intergender A term describing a person whose gender is in between *male* and *female*.

Intersex The state of having a body that naturally differs from what is usually expected of a male body or a female body in terms of its chromosomes, reproductive organs, secondary sexual characteristics or sex hormone balance. Being intersex is not the same as being transgender.

Misgender To describe a person using terms inappropriate to their gender (e.g. by referring to a trans man as *her*).

MTF Male to female – a person who has transitioned, is transitioning or intends to transition from a male gender role to a female gender role.

Mx A gender-neutral title (equivalent to *Mr, Mrs, Ms* or *Miss*).

Neutrois A term describing a person who does not have a personal sense of gender or whose personal sense of gender is neutral, neither male nor female.

Non-binary A term describing a person who does not identify as fully and consistently male or female. Often used as an umbrella term for a range of genders other than male or female.

Outing Making a person's transgender status or sexual orientation known to other people.

Pangender An adjective that describes people who feel they are all genders or have some aspects of all genders.

Per A gender-neutral title (equivalent to *Mr*, *Mrs*, *Ms* or *Miss*).

Protected characteristic A characteristic which entitles a person to protection under the Equality Act.

Public Sector Equality Duty A legal duty under the provisions of which public sector organisations must seek to eliminate discrimination, promote equality and foster good relations between people with and without characteristics protected under the Equality Act (2010).

Real-life experience A period of living full time in the planned future gender role, which may be a mandatory requirement before access to surgery is granted.

Top surgery Transition-related surgery performed on the chest in order to remove breast tissue or enhance breast development.

Transgender 1) An adjective used as an umbrella term to describe anybody whose experience of gender is different from what would commonly be expected based on the gender they were classed as at birth. 2) An adjective describing somebody who has gone through a transition from male to female or from female to male, or who intends to do so.

Trans A short form of *transgender*.

Trans* A short form of *transgender* which is specifically used as an umbrella term for all kinds of transgender people.

Transfeminine A term used to describe people categorised as male at birth who identify more with femininity; or to describe non-binary people who, while not identifying as female, identify as more feminine than masculine.

Transition The process of moving from one public gender identity to another, potentially (but not inevitably) incorporating elements of social, psychological, hormonal, surgical and legal change. Used as both a noun and a verb.

Transmasculine A term used to describe people categorised as female at birth who identify more with masculinity; or to describe non-binary people who, while not identifying as male, identify as more masculine than feminine.

Transphobia Prejudice or hostility towards transgender people.

Transsexual An adjective describing a person who has undergone, or who wishes to undergo, transition. Usually reserved for binary trans people and rarely used today as it has been largely superseded by *transgender*.

Transvestite A person who engages in cross-dressing. This word is sometimes seen as offensive so should be used only for people who say they are happy to be described that way.

Pronouns

Several alternative pronouns are used by non-binary people in place of *he*, *she* and their derivatives. The following table details some of the most common ones, with more familiar examples to provide context.

Nominative	Accusative	Possessive adjective	Possessive pronoun	Reflexive
he	him	his	his	himself
she	her	her	hers	herself
they	them	their	theirs	themselves*
zie	zie	zir	zirs	zirself
xe	xe	xir	xirs	xirself
sie	hir	hir	hirs	hirself
per	per	per	pers	perself
fae	faer	faer	faers	faerself
co	co	co	cos	coself
ey	em	eir	eirs	emself

*Sometimes when *they* is used as a singular pronoun, the reflexive form *themself* is preferred.

The linguistic terms here might sound confusing, but these pronouns are easy to use in practice. The following examples show how the elements in the above table can be applied in simple sentences:

Nominative: There *she* is.

Accusative: Look at *her*.

Possessive adjective: That's *her* desk.

Possessive pronoun: That desk is *hers*.

Reflexive: She chose that desk for *herself*.

Endnotes

1. Martin, C. and Ruble, D. (2004) 'Children's search for gender cues: Cognitive perspectives on gender development.' *Current Directions in Psychological Science 13*, 2, 67–70.

2. Kranz, G.S., Hahn, A., Kaufmann, U., Küblböck, M. *et al.* (2014) 'White matter microstructure in transsexuals and controls investigated by diffusion tensor imaging.' *Neuroscience 34*, 46, 15466–15475.

3. Ainsworth, C. (2015) 'Sex redefined.' *Nature 518*, 7539, 288–291.

4. House of Commons Women and Equalities Committee (2016) *Report on Transgender Equality: First Report of Session 2015–2016.* London: The Stationery Office. Available at www.publications. parliament.uk/pa/cm201516/cmselect/cmwomeq/390/390.pdf, accessed on 21 April 2017.

5. Bristol City Council (2014) *Social Isolation, Gender and Sexual Orientation: Research Findings Report.* Available at www.bristol. gov.uk/documents/20182/34732/Social%20isolation%20 gender%20and%20sexuality_0.pdf/2315753c-3459-45ac-833d-6f55bad91ad3, accessed on 21 April 2017.

6. Equality Act (2010). Available at www.legislation.gov.uk/ukpga/ 2010/15/contents, accessed on 11 May 2017.

7. Keogh, P., Reid, R. and Weatherburn, P. (2006) *Lambeth LGBT Matters: The Needs and Experiences of Lesbians, Gay Men, Bisexual and Trans Men and Women in Lambeth.* London: Sigma Research and Lambeth Borough Council Commission for Social Care Inspection.

8. Equinet European Network of Equality Bodies (2012) *Being Trans in the European Union: Analysis of the EU LGBT Survey Data.* Available at www.equineteurope.org/IMG/pdf/fra-2014-being-trans-eu-comparative_en.pdf, accessed on 21 April 2017.

9. Glen, F. and Hurrell, K. (2012) *Measuring Gender Identity.* Manchester: Equality and Human Rights Commission. Available at www.equalityhumanrights.com/sites/default/files/technical_note_final.pdf, accessed on 11 May 2017.

10. Diversity in the Workplace, Randstad Workmonitor wave 3, September 2015. Available at www.randstad.gr/editor/uploads/files/2015_Randstad_Q3.pdf, accessed on 11 May 2017.

11. Human Rights Campaign Foundation (2013) *The Cost of the Closet and the Rewards of Inclusion – why the Workplace Environment for LGBT People Matters to Employers.* Available at www.hrc.org/resources/the-cost-of-the-closet-and-the-rewards-of-inclusion, accessed on 21 April 2017.

12. United Nations Office of the High Commissioner for Human Rights (2011) *Guiding Principles on Business and Human Rights.* Available at www.unglobalcompact.org/library/2, accessed on 11 May 2017.

13. Equality Act (2010). Available at www.legislation.gov.uk/ukpga/2010/15/contents, accessed on 11 May 2017.

14. Equality Act (2010). Quoted from part 2, chapter 1, section 7. Available at www.legislation.gov.uk/ukpga/2010/15/section/7, accessed on 11 May 2017.

15. Equality and Human Rights Commission (2011) *Employment Statutory Code of Practice.* London: Her Majesty's Stationery Office. Available at www.equalityhumanrights.com/en/publication-download/employment-statutory-code-practice, accessed on 11 May 2017.

16. Equality Act (2010). Available at www.legislation.gov.uk/ukpga/2010/15/contents, accessed on 11 May 2017.

17. Governnment Equalities Office (2011) *Equality Act 2010: Specific duties to support the equality duty. What do I need to know? A quick start guide for public sector organisations.* Available at www.pfc.org.uk/pdf/specific-duties%20Nov%202011%20(2).pdf, accessed on 11 May 2017.

18. Sex Discrimination (Gender Reassignment) Regulations (Northern Ireland) (1999). Available at www.legislation.gov.uk/ nisr/1999/311/contents/made, accessed on 10 July 2017.

19. Sex Discrimination (Northern Ireland) Order (1976). Available at www.legislation.gov.uk/nisi/1976/1042/contents, accessed on 10 July 2017.

20. Gender Recognition Act (2004). Available at www.legislation.gov. uk/ukpga/2004/7/contents, accessed on 10 July 2017.

21. Equality and Human Rights Commission (2015) *Employment Statutory Code of Practice.* Available at www.equalityhumanrights. com/en/publication-download/employment-statutory-code-practice, accessed on 11 May 2017.

22. Companies Act (2006). Quoted from section 414C, paragraph 7. Available at www.legislation.gov.uk/ukdsi/2013/9780111540169/ regulation/3, accessed on 11 May 2017.

23. Directive 2014/95/EU of the European Parliament and of the Council of 22 October 2014. Available at http://eur-lex.europa.eu/ legal-content/EN/TXT/?uri=CELEX:32014L0095, accessed on 11 May 2017.

24. Totaljobs Trans Employee Experiences Survey (2016). Available at www.totaljobs.com/insidejob/trans-employee-survey-report-2016, accessed on 10 July 2017.

25. Marriage (Same Sex Couples) Act (2013). Available at www. legislation.gov.uk/ukpga/2013/30/contents/enacted/data.htm, accessed on 11 May 2017.

26. Equality Act (2010). Available at www.legislation.gov.uk/ukpga/ 2010/15/contents, accessed on 11 May 2017.

27. *Sheffield v. Air Foyle Charter Airlines Ltd.* [1998].

28. The European Court of Justice ruling on the European Equal Treatment Directive, 30 April 1996. Available at http://eur-lex.europa. eu/legal-content/EN/TXT/?uri=CELEX%3A61994CJ0013, accessed on 11 May 2017.

29. Equality Act (2010). Available at www.legislation.gov.uk/ukpga/ 2010/15/contents, accessed on 11 May 2017.

30. Gender Recognition Act (2004). Available at www.legislation.gov. uk/ukpga/2004/7/pdfs/ukpga_20040007_en.pdf, accessed on 11 May 2017.

31. United Nations (1948). *Universal Declaration of Human Rights.* Available at www.un.org/en/universal-declaration-human-rights, accessed on 11 May 2017.

32. Regulation (EU) 2016/679 of the European Parliament and of the Council of 27 April 2016 on the protection of natural persons with regard to the processing of personal data and on the free movement of such data, and repealing Directive 95/46/EC (General Data Protection Regulation). Available at http://eur-lex.europa.eu/legal-content/EN/TXT/?uri=CELEX%3A32016R0679, accessed on 10 July 2017.

33. Data Protection Act (1998). Available at www.gov.uk/data-protection/the-data-protection-act, accessed on 11 May 2017.

34. Equality and Human Rights Commission (2016) *Sex Discrimination.* Available at www.equalityhumanrights.com/en/advice-and-guidance/sex-discrimination, accessed on 21 April 2017.

35. For specific guidance on exceptions under the Equality Act, see the Equality and Human Rights Commission's *Services, Public Functions and Associations: Statutory Code of Practice.* Available at www.equalityhumanrights.com/sites/default/files/publication_pdf/servicescode_0.pdf, accessed on 21 April 2017.

36. Totaljobs (2016) *Totaljobs Trans Employee Experiences Survey 2016.* Available at www.totaljobs.com/insidejob/trans-employee-survey-report-2016, accessed on 21 April 2017.

37. Stepstone (2017). *Trans at Work.* Available at www.genrespluriels.be/IMG/pdf/stepstone-trans-at-work-be2017.pdf, accessed on 10 July 2017.

38. Independent Press Standards Organisation (2017). *Editor's Code of Practice.* Available at www.ipso.co.uk/editors-code-of-practice, accessed on 10 July 2017.

39. Equality Act (2010). Available at www.legislation.gov.uk/ukpga/2010/15/contents, accessed on 11 May 2017.

40. Totaljobs (2016) *Totaljobs Trans Employee Experiences Survey 2016.* Available at www.totaljobs.com/insidejob/trans-employee-survey-report-2016, accessed on 21 April 2017.

41. Protection from Harassment Act (1997). Available at www.legislation.gov.uk/ukpga/1997/40/contents, accessed on 10 July 2017.

42. Equality Act (2010). *Section 26.* Available at www.legislation.gov.
uk/ukpga/2010/15/contents, accessed on 10 July 2017.

43. Equality and Human Rights Commission (2011) *Employment
Statutory Code of Practice.* London: Her Majesty's Stationery Office.

44. Gamp, J. (2016) 'Lloyds Bank to be the first UK company to offer
transgender surgery as healthcare benefit.' *International Business
Times,* 7 May 2016.

45. Leong, T. (2014) 'Malaysian court scraps cross-dressing ban in
landmark decision.' *Reuters,* 7 November 2014.

46. Heavens, A. (2010) 'Sudan men fined over "indecent" fashion show
makeup.' *Reuters,* 8 December 2010.

47. Survey by Ipsos and the Williams Institute at UCLA Law School,
29 December 2016. Available at www.buzzfeed.com/lesterfeder/
this-is-how-23-countries-feel-about-transgender-rights?utm_
term=.ippkoXkgW#.kxldbMdkw, accessed on 11 May 2017.

48. Schildt, K. (2011) *Just One of the Guys? Transgender Men and the
Persistence of Gender Inequality.* Chicago: University of Chicago
Press.

49. Grant Thornton (2015) *Women in Business: The Value of Diversity.*
Available at www.grantthornton.ae/content/files/women-in-
business-value-of-diversity-uae.pdf, accessed on 21 April 2017.

50. Human Rights Campaign (2017). *LGBTQ Equality at the Fortune
500.* Available at www.hrc.org/resources/lgbt-equality-at-the-
fortune-500, accessed on 10 July 2017.

Further Information

If you want to find out more about how best to manage a workplace with trans employees, there are several helpful organisations you can turn to.

Advice on regulations

The **Information Commissioner's Office** has lots of useful advice on its website at https://ico.org.uk and runs a helpline on 0303 123 1113.

The **Equality and Human Rights Commission (EHRC)** offers useful advice on human rights and the Equality Act on its website at www.equalityhumanrights.com/en and you can call on 0808 800 0082. In Scotland, its sister organisation the **Scottish Human Rights Commission (SHRC)** can be found online at www.scottishhumanrights.com and telephoned on 0131 244 3550.

Acas has guidelines on issues around discrimination against trans employees on its website at www.acas.org.uk/index.aspx?articleid=2064 and has a helpline you can call on 0300 123 1100.

Sector-specific information

Government departments can find support on trans issues from the staff network **a:gender**, whose website is at www. agender.org.uk and who can be phoned on 0114 207 2547 or emailed at agender@homeoffice.gsi.gov.uk

The Law Society provides advice for legal firms working with trans employees on its website at www.lawsociety.org. uk/support-services/advice/practice-notes/working-with-transgender-employees

Schools dealing with a teacher who is transitioning at work can find best practice guidelines from the **Gender Identity Research and Education Society (GIRES)** in PDF form at www.gires.org.uk/assets/2017/Transition%20of%20 a%20Teacher%20in%20School.pdf

Health sector organisations can find useful advice on the **NHS Employers** website at www.nhsemployers.org/ your-workforce/plan/building-a-diverse-workforce/get-involved/celebrating-diversity/transgender

Police forces with transitioning staff can get advice from the **National Trans Police Association**, whose website is at www.ntpa.online – there is a contact form on the site.

Local trans organisations

The **LGBT Consortium** has a directory of local organisations across the UK on its website at www. lgbtconsortium.org.uk. If you can't find anything in your area, you can call 020 7064 6500 or email admin@ lgbtconsortium.org.uk for advice.

Training

Stonewall provides training on trans issues for businesses right across the UK. You can find their website at www. stonewall.org.uk or call 020 7593 1850 for information. Their email address is info@stonewall.org.uk

The **Equality Network** provides training to businesses in Scotland through the **Scottish Transgender Alliance**. You can read about what they have to offer on their website at www.scottishtrans.org/our-work/training or call them on 0131 467 6039. They have two email addresses – sta@ equality-network.org or info@scottishtrans.org – either of which you can contact for advice.

London-based organisation **Galop** offers training on LGBT issues which is fully inclusive of trans issues. You can read about it on their website at www.galop.org.uk/ training or call them on 020 7704 6767. Their services manager, Peter Kelley, can be emailed at peter@galop.org. uk

GenderAgenda provides training across a range of trans issues. You can find an extensive set of resources on their website at www.genderagenda.net and they can be telephoned on 0844 808 3699.

General information about trans people

US LGBTI organisation **GLAAD** has a useful set of tips for people who want to support trans people on its website at www.glaad.org/transgender/allies

The **NHS** has information on trans healthcare issues on its website at www.nhs.uk/LiveWell/Transhealth/Pages/ Transhealthhome.aspx

PwC, which has been a pioneer in supporting trans people in its offices, has a guide which draws on its experiences available on its website at gender.bitc.org.uk/all-resources/case-studies/transgender-policies-pwc

Unison provides advice on trans people and employment discrimination on its website at www.unison.org.uk/get-help/knowledge/discrimination/transgender-discrimination

Trans Media Watch is media-focused but has information that may be useful in other industries, including a guide to speaking and writing about trans people respectfully, on its website at www.transmediawatch.org/media.html

Index

Jennie Kermode MA (hons) MRes is Chair of Trans Media Watch, a charity promoting positive media representations of the transgender community. She has written for the *Independent*, the *New Statesman*, *Pink News* and *New Internationalist*, and is a commissioning editor at Eye For Film. She has provided training on trans issues for private and public sector organisations and has worked with government on initiatives aimed at tackling transphobic hate crime.